the
DRAGON
net

the
DRAGON
net

How God Has Used Communism to Prepare
China for the Gospel

Silas Hong

Fleming H. Revell Company
Old Tappan, New Jersey

Unless otherwise identified, Scripture quotations in this volume are from the King James Version of the Bible.

Scripture quotations identified LB are from The Living Bible, Copyright © 1971 by Tyndale House Publishers, Wheaton, Illinois 60187. All rights reserved.

The Church in Communist China by Francis Price Jones © 1962 Friendship Press, New York. Used by permission.

Christianity in Communist China by George N. Patterson, © 1969. Used by permission of Word Books, Publishers, Waco, Texas.

Excerpts from *Come Wind, Come Weather* by Leslie T. Lyall. Copyright 1960. Moody Press, Moody Bible Institute of Chicago. Used by permission.

Excerpts from *The Chinese Church That Will Not Die* by Mary Wang. Used by permission of Tyndale House Publishers, Wheaton, Illinois 60187.

Library of Congress Cataloging in Publication Data

Hong, Silas.
    The dragon net.

    Includes bibliographical references.
      1. Christianity—China. 2. Missions—China.
3. China—Religion. 4. Communism and Christianity—
China. I. Title.
BR1285.H65   266'.00951   75-33773
ISBN 0-8007-0775-3

To **Deanne**, my wife and inspiration, whose encouragement, helpful suggestions and dedicated efforts in taking dictation on the typewriter made this work possible.

Contents

Introduction   9

1 Speaking of Facts. . . .   13
2 Theistic Population Explosion   28
3 The Takeover   35
4 The Gates of Hell   54
5 Language Reform and Evangelism   80
6 Psyched Out. . . .   91
7 The Dragon Changes Spots   110
8 Pressing Toward the Mark   122

Notes   127

Introduction

On October 1, 1974, China celebrated her twenty-fifth anniversary of the founding of the People's Republic. Forty-five hundred guests from all five continents representing eighty countries showed up at the gala occasion. The Chinese Party leaders and their comrades entertained them as the five-star red flags fluttered in the breeze under the Peking sky.

During this glorious festival of the socialist motherland, the People's Republic boasted:

> Under the wise leadership of the Chinese people's great leader, Chairman Mao . . . China has become more consolidated than ever . . . we have friends all over the world. The situation at home and abroad is excellent.[1]

So it seems, in the eyes of the world, that a godless regime has successfully and triumphantly traversed twenty-five years of militant course, while her counterpart, Taiwan, becomes increasingly unpopular. One gains a seat in the United Nations as the other loses face. One constantly receives additional recognition and the other reduces the number of embassies around the world. How long is this going to continue? What lies ahead for China? How does this all relate to the Gospel of Jesus Christ?

After speaking to a college group in the San Francisco Bay area on the subject of Christianity in China, a young student told me that his professor had assured him there are no more Christians in the Middle Kingdom. He said that Mao has been successful in totally annihilating Christianity within that vast land.

Is this truly the state of the Church of God on the mainland? Has the Lord Almighty been defeated? Are the labors of thousands of missionaries in vain? And what about the prayers of the saints? Ever since the takeover, God's children have prayed for the day when the Lord would deliver His own on the mainland. Were they all beating the air?

No! Absolutely not! It is this writer's belief that God has a divine plan for China. Just as He used the Egyptians, Canaanites, Amorites, Hittites, and Jebusites and all the other godless forces to mold His own people, He has used Communism to fulfill His divine will in China. As Psalms 76:10 reminds us, "Surely the wrath of man shall praise [God]. . . ." Mao may think those five-year plans were his own brainchild, but in reality they were carried out only because God permitted it. Proverbs 21:1 (LB) verifies this:

> Just as water is turned into irrigation ditches, so the Lord directs the king's thoughts. He turns them wherever he wants to.

In this book I am letting the events speak for themselves. These facts clearly reveal the fingerprints of God when dusted with truth. They substantiate without a shadow of a doubt that the Lord of history has always had a divine hand upon China.

In Hudson Taylor's autobiographical writings, he told of his experience in China in the following words:

> We were to prove . . . that these circumstances which seemed so trying were necessary links in the chain of a divinely ordered providence guiding to other and wider spheres.[2]

Those words, uttered nearly 120 years ago by that giant among missionaries, who dedicated his entire life to China, proved to be prophetically and emphatically true.

the
DRAGON
net

I

Speaking of Facts. . . .

Who in times past suffered all nations to walk in their
own ways. Nevertheless he left not himself without wit-
ness. . . .

Acts 14:16, 17

It was a perfect day for the fifty-mile ride from Wanganui to Otaki. The rich green pastures and the spotless blue sky of the north island of New Zealand inspired me to roll down the car window and enjoy the smogless fresh air.

Around four-thirty that afternoon, my driver and I arrived at the church where I was to deliver a message on China that evening. It was a busy church. They had just finished their week-long conference and the children were helping their teachers tidy up the gymnasium. The congenial pastor greeted us with a very warm handshake and received us into his study. He assured me that special brochures and invitations were mailed out to many in the area, and especially to all the Chinese families in the community. He told me they were looking forward to a full house.

Good News From a Far Country

While I was meditating in the garden observing two pet sheep grazing leisurely, my companion handed me a telegram message he had just received over the phone. The note stated that word had just reached the New Zealand office that an entire village located on the southeastern coast of China had accepted Jesus Christ as their personal Saviour and Lord. It went on to say that out of the one hundred eighty new converts, eighty followed up in baptism.

Wow! That was some news. News I had longed to hear. It was like cool water to a thirsty soul and a superenergy shot to a tired body. It made my whole trip!

Immediately all the weariness which had been accumulating during my past two weeks of touring the island left me. "This is what it's all about," I told myself. "This makes all the efforts worthwhile."

Upon arriving home in Los Angeles, I learned from the headquarters of Underground Evangelism that the miraculous conversion began when the headman in the village was saved. He then proceeded to witness to his fellow villagers, and soon a complete victory was won.

Today the little village holds regular Bible study sessions while guards watch out for danger from local authorities.

What a glorious harvest this was—and all because forty-five gospel booklets penetrated the Bamboo Curtain.

Are you surprised at this thrilling outcropping of God's power? Do you think it is impossible? Well, here are a few more encouraging testimonies of the Holy Spirit at work there.

More Good News

When I was speaking in Australia at a united church rally, a young Chinese came to me after the service to say he had just received a letter from his relative on the mainland encouraging him to walk closely with the Lord. He was pleasantly surprised the writer dared to say such things under a watchful atheistic eye. But, my beloved, the people on the mainland are not carbon copies of their government, behaving mechanically like Marxist-Leninist robots. There are 800 million *individuals* in China.

After Bernard Barron, World Vision's Director of Projects in Canada, returned from a visit to China, he reported that the Christian Church there, though small and low-profile, is strong. He said the young people are either gripped by "new religion" or are dissatisfied. They testify to each other, adopting a missionary air and are now patiently expounding an axiomatically faultless gospel, preaching the Word with proselytizing fervor.

A twenty-four-year-old Christian refugee testified in a World Vision interview about the great opportunity for evangelism in China and that he himself had led six to the Lord.

A returning visitor reported the Church was dynamic with Christians witnessing and worshiping. Five of his closest childhood friends had been won to Christ during the past two years.

Journalist Bell quoted a young Christian woman in *Eternity Magazine* in September, 1972:

> While Richard Nixon crossed the snow-mantled square of the Old Imperial Palace in Peking last February . . . a small group of Christians gathered in a remote Chinese mountain village and worshipped Jesus, the God of all reality.

The Modern New Testament Church

There is and always has been a living Church in the Middle Kingdom since the Communist takeover. Dr. Dick Hillis says that he is convinced that in mainland China there is a "church of the catacombs," and that God certainly has His people there in secret cells of believers quietly maintaining fellowship with God and with one another.

It is a well-substantiated fact that many cell groups, averaging eight to ten people, meet regularly. Impromptu meetings are also arranged while two or three believers are sitting on a park bench, waiting in the train station, or simply strolling along.

Victor Hayward commented in the *Church Times,* December 14, 1973, regarding an interview with a young Christian refugee from China: "The Christians," she said, "meet clandestinely, sometimes in the open, in woods or among the hills, but never in the same place, and sometimes in small groups in homes. . . ."

There can be no question that the Church of our Lord Jesus Christ is marching on in the Mainland. It is an indigenous, independent, pure, and powerful witness of God. She is not concerned with denominations. She is only dedicated to worshiping and serving the living God.

According to J. D. James's article in the *Moody Monthly*

magazine in March, "Although China's doors are considered closed yet, more evangelistic work has been done in the past twenty-five years in China than in the previous two-hundred years."

At the Southern Baptist Convention in Miami Beach during June of 1975, the executive secretary of their foreign missions board, Baker J. Cauthen, a former China missionary, made this enlightening statement to his 15 thousand listeners: "There are more believers in China today than there were when missionaries had to come out."

Gospel Portions Delivered . . . in China

Several months ago I received a report from Hong Kong telling me about the conversion of a young man in China. It said that he became a Christian because an elderly lady was able to present him with a gospel pamphlet. The young man read the booklet and was converted as a result. Later he escaped to Hong Kong and told his story to my friends there.

Eyewitness News

If you are still doubtful of the Christian activities in the Middle Kingdom, then permit me to recount the experience of three young Chinese ladies who visited their homeland with a missionary purpose. As they stepped off the train in Canton late last year, they searched diligently for a hotel to no avail. Finally, a vacancy in a rundown inn on the outskirts of town was located and they decided to bunk down for the night.

The next morning they got up early and asked the old inn-keeper how to find a certain address which they had memorized. The elderly gentleman looked at them and inquired in a soft voice, "Are you girls Christians?" Surprised at the question, they were speechless for a moment. Not wishing to deny Christ, one brave girl replied, "Yes, we are Christians." Then to their amazement and joy the old man whispered back, "So am I."

Thus far you have witnessed only a few of the more exciting, more dramatic events. God is doing a hundred times more in China today. For example, one personal friend who just returned from his second visit to China told me many, many encouraging things. True, these events did not make the headlines. Perhaps their significance will never be told in full. Nevertheless, the Spirit of God is working through His children in a mysterious way to win many to the Lord.

Trading the Red Flag for the Shed Blood

Inside the great wall of atheism, not only many average citizens are finding themselves in the Lord; even some Communist officers are experiencing rebirth today.

In a commune of two thousand people there was a young, dedicated officer in charge who was anxious to do a good job for the Party. He made certain that everyone had his daily work to do and that they carried out their proper tasks. In the course of time, he discovered there was one person who was rather different, smiling and cheerful at work.

One day, pressed by the feeling of annoyance and intrigue, he pulled the fellow aside and demanded, "Say Comrade, what are you trying to prove? You are always smiling and happy at work even when I give you the dirtiest job to do. I have heard reports that you have been telling people about God, about Jesus Christ, and about salvation. Comrade, we are Communists! We don't believe in God, or Jesus Christ, or salvation. And furthermore I am sick and tired of your nonsense! I order you to stop this behavior or I will be forced to take action."

The young Christian listened carefully and then replied, "I understand your position, but may I ask you a simple personal question? Are you happy? I mean, are you really happy?"

"Am I happy? What do you mean, 'Am I happy?' " he shouted. "I am a Communist—I don't have to be happy!"

Then because the young man pressed for an answer, the officer retorted as he stomped away, "It's none of your business!"

That night, while the Christian was sleeping, there came a tug on his pillow. As he opened his eyes, he saw the young officer standing by the bed motioning to him with a whisper, "Come with me." The sudden development found the Christian sleepy, puzzled, and fearful; for you see, thousands in China had vanished in the darkness of the night. Their shadows disappeared in the night air and were never seen again. Nevertheless, the young man got up and followed him.

Outside in the privacy and coolness of the midnight air something extraordinary took place. The young officer confessed to the Christian that he was miserably unhappy. He wanted to learn his secret of happiness.

With thanksgiving overflowing from his heart, the Christian shared, "Jesus Christ makes me happy. Jesus Christ makes the difference. You know, you can be just as happy as I am if you only receive Him as your Personal Saviour and Lord."

To the honor and glory of God, the young Christian and the officer knelt down together in the moonlight and called on the name of the Lord.

Greater Love Hath No Man. . . .

It's happening! The evidence of the power of God not only is proven in the foregoing dynamic fashion, it also revealed itself in the free world. Not too long ago a friend of mine was speaking in a church in Hong Kong. Sitting in the congregation was a fifteen-year-old girl who weighed about ninty pounds. From the way she looked, he realized immediately that she had been through something horrible. So after the service he engaged her in a word of conversation and learned she had escaped from China only two days prior to that meeting. She told him it took her several hours of swimming in the cold water while the communist searchlights were crisscrossing all around her.

There she was, two days after her survival swim, still tired, afraid and shivering, worshiping in the house of the Lord.

Impressed by her dramatic recent experience, my friend invited her to come to the office to see the gospels printed in the new Mao script. When she got a hold of the first copy, she began weeping uncontrollably. As she turned around and saw the stack of gospel portions on the table, she said, "Assuming God gives me the strength, would you mind giving me fifteen of these copies? I want to swim back and share the Word of God with my friends!"

The New Look

Tremendous changes are taking place inside China today.

The Christian Church is again open. Christmas caroling was heard once more, and the cell-group gatherings can be conducted in a much less secretive atmosphere.

Look at the change taking place on the borders. Many travelers have been allowed to go in and come out. Communist officers have permitted one or two Bibles or a few pieces of Christian literature to pass the inspection at the border of Hong Kong and Canton.

Notice also the daily hour-long Shanghai broadcasts of English language instruction and the launching of additional training in English throughout the mainland. Not too long ago one million freshly printed English-language teaching textbooks were sold out in three days.

As you may have guessed, these changes have not taken place accidentally. It isn't just the result of the easing off of the official attitude. Nor is it only because China had to oblige the Western world in order to secure its aid. These obvious reasons are simply the result of God's planning and guidance.

The Fingerprints of God

It is evident that God has a plan for China. It is embedded even in the Chinese characters. Let's look at this word 來 meaning *come.* Since the Chinese characters are constructed with strokes which often form subwords, it is interesting to note that this particular character is made up of two subwords, *cross* 十 and *man* 人 . It shows a cross and three men; the big man on the middle cross and two small men on each side. Doesn't this suggest the Crucifixion story?

Once a Chinese student challenged me on the interpretation

by pointing out that it was not exactly a cross because the vertical stroke has a small upward turn at the bottom. "Well," I replied, "that little turn is the genius of the Holy Spirit, my friend. It is the symbol of the spike which lay at the foot of the cross. It is there to remind you of the pain that Christ suffered as He hung there."

To continue in this remarkable line, take a look at the character 舟 meaning *ship*. The forming of this character is extremely biblical to say the least. On the left there is the character for *boat* 舟 and on the right *eight* 八 and *mouth* 口 . This word illustrates eight people and a boat. Who is to say that it does not convey the story of Noah's ark?

Why were these words constructed with such obvious biblical flavor? Were they only to show the universality of the Flood and the renown of the Crucifixion? Or are they in fact evidence of God's hold upon the Chinese race?

It Is Written. . . .

As we turn to the Word itself, we discover even more interesting clues. For instance, in Matthew 13:3–9 (LB) the Lord uttered a parable regarding the sower and the soils. He said:

> "A farmer was sowing grain in his fields. As he scattered the seed across the ground, some fell beside a path, and the birds came and ate it. And some fell on rocky soil where there was little depth of earth; the plants sprang up quickly enough in the shallow soil, but the hot sun soon scorched them and they withered and died, for they had so little root. Other seeds fell among thorns, and the thorns choked out the tender blades. But some fell on good soil, and produced a crop that was thirty, sixty, and even a hundred times as much as he had planted. If you have ears, listen!"

Based on Christ's explanation of the parable in the nineteenth verse of the same chapter, it is obvious that He meant to describe four kinds of people and their reactions to the Word. Isn't it interesting that these four situations of seed-sowing paralleled the four major evangelistic thrusts directed toward China between 635 and 1948?

Nestorians

In the seventh century, the Nestorians came from Syria to spread the Christian faith. The famous Nestorian Monument reveals that the virtuous priest Olopuen arrived in China at Changan (now Sian in Shensi) during the resplendent, prosperous T'ang dynasty.

With the cooperation of the brilliant Emperor T'ai-tsung, preparations were made for translation of the Scriptures in the Imperial Library. Subsequent to three years' deep involvement in the study of the true Sutras, a proclamation was issued in the month of the twelve Chang-Kwan year to give the movement a free course throughout the land.

Nestorianism quickly gained momentum with the conversion of influential people such as Kuo-Tzu-i, the supreme commander of the army and chief minister of the state. Kuo contributed large sums of money for church building like the Ta-Tsung monastery which was built in the Ward of Repose.

By the time Emperor Kao-tsung (650–683) succeeded to his father's throne, monasteries were erected in every one of the prefectures. As Olopuen continued to find favor in the eyes of the emperor and was raised to be the Lord of the Great Law, Protector of the Empire, monasteries filled a hundred cities.

However, this first evangelistic attempt was only a superficial one. It only reached the Chinese elite. Very much like the seeds sown by the wayside, it established no roots and soon attracted the attention of the fowls.

Birds of a Feather

The first bird to swoop down was in the form of Buddhism. It might be called the "bird in the priestly robe." Those Buddhists who had established themselves centuries earlier hurled fabrications, allegations, and the like at the Nestorians in an attempt to snatch the seeds away.

The second bird who tried to steal the seed was dressed in the empress's gown. A bigoted woman, Empress Wu, lashed out all her fury and jealousy against her enemy with her extraordinary ability and daring.

Finally, in the year 845, Emperor Wu-tsung, who was a slave to all the superstitions, plainly declared an edict against religions of foreign nations. He ordered more than three thousand religious teachers to resume the ways of ordinary life and cease their "unsubstantial talkings."

Although the Nestorian movement gained some ground in China and earned the name *Ching Chiao* (luminous or great religion), the reversal of Christ's law ". . . to the poor the gospel is preached . . ." limited its influence. Consequently when the tidal wave of persecution swept over them, the initial movement was devoured by the fowls. Two hundred and ten years of effort came to a complete halt.

Franciscans

After more than three hundred fifty years of silence the Italians under the Franciscan Mission came to propagate Christendom in the middle of the thirteenth century. The comeback took place when Kublai Khan established his kingdom in central China and formed the Yuen dynasty.

The Mongol Empire's tolerance of religion and their eagerness to absorb external ideas inspired the Pope to establish the work in Peking. So Giovanni di Monte Corvino was sent to further the faith in the East.

Like his predecessors, Giovanni di Monte Corvino began his work by first gaining the confidence of the ruling class. He took under his protection about 150 boys from the elite of society from seven through eleven years old and educated them in the Christian faith in Greek and Latin. They were also employed to write psalters and Christian literature.

Under Monte Corvino's supervision the boys became quite efficient, and some of them were able to carry on the services on their own. Furthermore, some of the boys were chosen to form a special choir, and their performance was regularly enjoyed by the emperor.

At the end of his twenty-year endeavor Giovanni di Monte Corvino had baptized six hundred people.

The Scorching Sun

His rather swift accomplishment aroused the jealousy of other religious figures. Giovanni di Monte Corvino was tried as a spy and deceiver of men. It was the confession of the accuser, a Nestorian priest, which finally cleared his name.

Although Monte Corvino was elevated by the Pope to be the Archbishop and Patriarch of the whole East, he felt the intense heat of loneliness. The Pope's numerous attempts to send helpers to assist him in his increasing responsibilities were futile. Groups of missionary friars were swallowed up by the long hazardous journey to the vast East.

When Monte Corvino died in 1328, the Franciscan missionary effort vanished also. This second major attempt only touched the upper class. Its main converts were the Mongols who then ruled the Middle Kingdom. The stony ground had taken its toll.

Jesuits

It was not until over two hundred years later that the third major evangelistic attempt was mobilized by the Jesuits from Spain. This movement was made possible at the beginning of the sixteenth century because merchants came from Portugal and Spain to trade with the Chinese in the southern part of the empire. The opportunity, that the tradesmen's activities afforded, awakened the missionaries in Europe to the long-forgotten dream of converting the masses in China.

Due to the xenophobian control, the first attempts of this movement were carried out under tremendous difficulty. However, the dedicated Jesuits such as Matteo Ricci and Michele Ruggieri were able eventually to win the hearts of the Chinese people with their knowledge of math, geography, astronomy, and fluency in the Chinese tongue.

Upon gaining a foothold, the Jesuits devised a different approach for themselves. They tried to reach the native people in their own language and allowed local leadership to develop.

Soon Ricci became a reputable scholar and gained a number
of converts. His fame then reached the ears of the emperor,
who gave him permission to build churches in several cities.
When Kang Hsi came to the throne the Jesuits not only ex-
tended their work through the provinces, but also became personal friends, physicians, and counselors to the emperor. They
were placed at the head of the most important offices of the
state.

In order to successfully propagate their ministry, the Jesuits
set up systematic training programs for the Chinese. They ordained some of them as priests and consecrated one as bishop.
Work proceeded well. The fifteen Jesuit missionaries who la-
bored in China between the years 1581–1600 increased to 210 by
the 1700s. A quarter of a century later the Jesuits had three
hundred churches and claimed a membership of 300 thousand.

Thorns and Thistles

Their successful evangelistic thrust was made possible because they penetrated the grass roots. Nevertheless, the seeds
fell into the thorns. The thorn of contention grew to choke the
movement when a native of Chekiang by the name of Sun
protested against the Jesuit effort to reform the Chinese calendar. Later another prickle in the guise of K. S. Young pierced
the Jesuits on three grounds: (1) He accused them of secretly
planning agitation. (2) He claimed they were guilty of teaching
the people evil lies. (3) He said they incorrectly arranged the
calendar.

Among the nettles grew one large bristle known as the Emperor's Decree of 1704 over the Rites Controversy. This completely severed the relationship between the Pope and the
emperor and resulted in the temporary dissolving of the Society
of Jesus Christ by Pope Clement XIV in 1773. (And the movement sank into near extinction.) As the Scripture states, the
thorns sprang up and choked them.

Protestantism

Finally, in the nineteenth century, God moved Robert Morrison to come to China. His arrival on September 4, 1807 in Canton is the beginning of the Protestant missionary era.

Unlike the Nestorians and Franciscans, Morrison did not set his goal on reaching the emperor and elite of the Chinese nation. His first attempt was directed to a lowly shop worker named Tsae-a-ko. Before he baptized him in 1814, his efforts were concentrated on the translation of the Bible.

Although his personal evangelistic efforts drew only about ten Chinese converts in his twenty years of continuous effort, he was able to complete the translation work with the help of his colleague, William Milne.

When Morrison died on August 1, 1834, the seed had already taken root in the good ground and produced much good fruit, such as the Chinese evangelist Leong Farr.

Counting the Fruit

During the nineteenth century the Protestant mission expanded by leaps and bounds. By 1890 there were more than 22 societies and 1280 missionaries in China. Churches, schools, hospitals, and orphanages spread throughout the cities. In the 1930s the good seeds had produced 567,000 converts, 600 primary schools, 265 junior high and high schools, 13 Christian universities and 2196 ordained Chinese ministers.

As you rejoice in this thirty-fold and sixty-fold harvest, don't forget to include these. It profoundly influenced China's leaders, Dr. Sun Yat-sen and Generalissimo Chiang Kai-shek. It inspired the establishment of the True Jesus Church in 1917, the Jesus Family in 1921, and the Little Flock in 1926. It also produced spiritual giants like John Sung, Wang Ming-tao, and Watchman Nee.

Looking Ahead

The parable of seed-sowing refers to fruit thirty-, sixty-, and one hundred-fold. So far only the first two figures are accounted for. What about the last figure? Are we going to see the result of a hundred-fold?

In spite of all Mao's efforts to wipe out completely the Christian faith in the past twenty-five years, he only succeeded in destroying the visible and tangible things of the Church. It is true that he closed all the churches during the Cultural Revolution. It is true that he burned thousands and thousands of Scriptures. It is also true that he forced the servants of the Lord to kneel on the ground and watch their beloved books burn. But it is equally true that he was never able to uproot the Christian life itself. The seeds continue to grow. The Word of God and the Church of our Lord Jesus Christ not only survived through the twenty-five years of atheistic Communism; it will certainly produce a hundred-fold harvest.

More Witnesses

It sounds too dogmatic? Well, it is this writer's privilege to interview many recent refugees, escapees, and returning visitors from the mainland. Among them was a young girl whom I met recently. From our in-depth conversation, I was reassured once again that the Church in China is very much alive. This young lady related her experience of meeting with fourteen other Christians in a believer's home. They shared their testimonies and prayed for and with each other. Tears trickled down the faces of the believers when they saw the Bible she had brought with her. Weeping over a copy of the Bible? Yes, because it was the first complete Bible they had seen for a long, long time. The young girl passed the Bible around and each one of the fourteen believers stained the pages with their tears of joy.

During my recent stay in the Orient, many young refugees testified to the fact that there are numerous cell groups on the mainland. They have seen with their own eyes how Christians worship, witness independently, secretly, and consistently under the guidance of the Holy Spirit and the protection of Almighty God.

Focusing a Point

Communists may think that they have defeated the Lord because they closed the churches and burned the Bibles; but God is still high on the throne. He was in control of the situation when He allowed the seed to be sown, to grow, and to multiply. He is in control today. He will also be in control in the future. In fact, we must realize that everything done inside China is within His divine plan. He is the Lord of history and Master of mankind!

For years the question of why God allowed Communism to prevail in China has deeply disturbed me. My special concern was caused by the fact I was virtually kicked out of the country as Mao's forces advanced. Consequently, in search of the answer I longed for, I began to study, pray, search, and research.

Finally, God granted the answer: *God has used twenty-five years of Communism on the mainland of China to prepare her for a massive evangelism program yet to be seen by the entire world.* Yes, there shall come a day when a hundred-fold harvest will be seen as thousands and thousands of Chinese men and women, boys and girls will cry unto the Lord for salvation.

Mao doesn't know it, but he has been helping set the stage. Proverbs 20:24 shows that, "Man's goings are of the Lord; how can a man then understand his own way?" A close look at China's own religions will show why this needed to happen.

2

Theistic Population Explosion

What profiteth the graven image that the maker thereof hath graven it; the molten image, and a teacher of lies, that the maker of his work trusteth therein, to make dumb idols?

Habakkuk 2:18

For in that day every man shall cast away his idols of silver, and his idols of gold, which your own hands have made unto you for a sin.

Isaiah 31:7

As a little boy traveling through China with my parents, I remember encountering a vast number of gods in the various provinces and cities. There were the god of mercy, the god of beggars, the goddess of the sea, the kitchen god, the monkey god, river god, mountain god, and an endless list of other carved and graven images. If you add ancestor worship, Buddhism, Taoism, and Confucianism to this almost unlimited legion, you can see why incense was such big business!

Ancestor Worship

I shall never forget the time my father took the family to visit his birthplace, the Hong village, in the province of Chekiang. In addition to riding cows and swimming in the creek, I visited the "ancestor hall." As we entered the big cold building, an extremely heavy odor of incense overwhelmed me. My mind quickly recalled the time Gramma took me shopping in one of the numerous incense stores where I saw wall-to-wall candles, incense sticks, and intriguing paper articles.

Father led me past several tables ladened with wooden plaques bearing the names and dates of the births and deaths of our ancestors. As we stopped in front of my grandfather's tablet, he asked me to plant the burning incense stick in the small burner in front of it and bow my head in respect. I followed the order but wondered why a man like my dad, who claimed no fear of either god or devil, would bow before his ancestor.

This introduction to ancestor worship gave me a warm sense of belonging when I was told that these departed ancestors (and even our unborn descendants) have a constant influence on our lives. As I looked around at the others in the hall, I understood better why they, too, came to such an unfriendly place.

Later I discovered that this practice was not confined to the "halls." Often a special place in the home was designated as the "family shrine" where a small cabinet on a pedestal housed a wooden tablet. In addition to the name and dates inscribed on the plaque, two words always appeared prominently. They were 神位—"seat of the spirit."

The establishment of the shrine was usually the eldest son's responsibility. At the death of his parent, he or the one officiating the ceremony would first pray at the grave, "Let the bones and flesh return to the earth, and may the spirit reside with us in the tablet." Later at home, he would take a brush (the Chinese *pen*) and paint a single stroke on top of the character 王 (king) to make it 主 (Lord). By adding this one dot, it is believed they instigate the spirit of the departed to dwell in the tablet, thus making him a guest in the home.

On special occasions I participated in the rite called Sweeping the Tomb. During the spring, the family carried boiled chicken, pork, vegetables, and fruits along with incense and candles to the ancestor's grave. There the incense and candles were burned and food displayed in ceremonial dishes to pay respect and show concern for the deceased. Then, to make sure nothing was overlooked, we burned paper "money" and paper "gold and silver taels" (much like paper-mache) to insure the ancestor was well taken care of. It was not unusual for some families to go all out by offering paper rickshaws, houses, and even furniture (these were bamboo structures covered with colorful paper).

At the conclusion of the ritual, we would begin the spring cleaning. That's probably why the term "tomb sweeping" was adopted.

Ancestor worship is the most deeply rooted of all Chinese religious observances. Not only is it the base of Chinese social and religious institutions, it has the sanction of antiquity and the seal of the greatest Chinese sages. It isn't surprising that six million sterling was lavished on building the mausoleum for the Father of China, Dr. Sun Yat-sen.

Nature Worship

During our stay in the Hong village, I caught a cold and developed a sore throat. Since doctors were few and far between, my concerned grandmother prescribed a "cure." She instructed my uncle to take me to a huge tree at the river's fork to pray and burn incense to the god who lived there. Then he was to mix the incense ashes with river water in a small cup for me to drink. Needless to say, I found that hard to swallow and subsequently refused.

Grandmother wasn't very happy with me that day. She assured all of us that the god of the tree had cured many who sincerely sought him. I was too young to argue but old enough to detect her apparent faith in the tree god.

Her attitude is a perfect illustration of Chinese pantheism. Many villagers, and even some city dwellers, would pray to the mountain or river for one reason or another. This polytheistic faith was typical of the Chinese culture.

Buddha Worship

My lessons in "religious education" were not yet over. Weeks later, when we arrived in Hangchow, my mother's hometown, I had the dubious privilege of accompanying my gramma on one of her visits to a massive Buddhist temple. She handed me two sticks of incense as we entered the main hall filled with idols of all sorts so I could pay homage to the gods. After bowing before many tall figures, including the black-faced and red-faced gods, we joined others in prostrating before the large frightening Buddha. I kept my eyes firmly closed during Gramma's long prayer and was too scared to let go of her hand. It seemed a long time before we left, and I hoped I would never have to go through that again. However, the constant appearance of Buddhist temples in every province we visited proved otherwise.

The fact that Buddhism became so absorbed into the Chinese culture after its introduction from India in the first century A.D. is very unique. Why was Buddhism able to become a Chinese religion while Christianity and other religions remained foreign? Let's take a look and see.

Buddhism originated with a man called Gotama who lived during Ezekiel's and Daniel's lifetimes near Kapilavastu on the border of Nepal. The title Buddha, which means The Enlightened or Awakened One, was given him because he produced the Four Truths at the culmination of his prolonged meditation. The essence of his message, which later developed into Theravada (Southern Buddhism) and Mahayana (Northern Buddhism), was that cessation of suffering could be achieved if one ceases to desire or crave selfishly. In the canon of the Theravada, called the Three Pitakas (which by the way is eleven times the size of the Bible), the radical system of self-deliverance unfolded.

To the Middle Kingdom which had seen her share of suffering and hardship, this seemed too good to be true! Here was a humanistic and rationalistic system to eliminate one of the most negative aspects of life. It meant Utopia was just around the corner. What an appetizing bait! That's why China, who considered herself the superior race and center of the world, swallowed her national pride and Buddhism along with it.

Confucianism and Taoism

The last time you sat down to a twelve-course Chinese banquet, chances are you were completely unaware of the profound influence Confucianism and Taoism had on your dinner.

Confucius, who lived during 551–478 B.C. was a philosopher and a gourmet. Among other things, he dealt with the standard of culinary arts and established rules for food preparation. This ancient Chinese sage placed strong emphasis on enjoyment of taste. He said, "There is no man who does not eat and drink but there are few who can appreciate taste."

The texture, appearance, and flavor of the food were Confucius's main concern. He wanted his rice polished white and his meats properly marinated and minced. It is said that he would not touch stale or tasteless food and would even refuse to sit down if the table were not properly set.

On the other hand, Lao-tsze (the founder of Taoism) who lived during 604–531 B.C., concerned himself with the more obscure aspects of food—its hygiene and nutritional values. He looked for simplicity and believed that longevity could be achieved by a simple life through the life-giving attributes of the diet. The you-are-what-you-eat philosophy was his.

It was believed that the tea ceremony could lead one into the quiet contemplation of the simple beauties of life. He taught that tea drinking can leave behind all worldly concern and lead into a moment of sanity and serenity.

These contrasting philosophies competed with each other for six centuries, taking deep root in every aspect of Chinese culture like salt and pepper. Their writings (*Annals of Lu,* "Spring and Autumn," *The Five Classics,* and the *Four Books* by Confucius; and the *Tao-teh-Ching* by Lao-tsze) were basically responsible for the widespread Chinese idolatry.

When Christianity came along with the message about the one true God and the only Saviour, Jesus Christ, no wonder it didn't become indigenous.

Go East, Young Man

When missionaries entered China, they were confronted with the monstrous pantheistic and polytheistic system that proved too great an adversary. For this reason, the Nestorians had to call it quits for 370 years after their initial evangelistic drive. Likewise, the Franciscans retreated for more than a century and a half after they were first expelled. The Jesuits fared little better, because Pope Clement XIV finally dissolved the movement in 1773.

It was also due to this tenacious Chinese resistance that Robert Morrison succeeded in winning only about ten converts after twenty years of faithful service.

True, statistics showed one million Protestants and three million Catholics in 1949 when Mao made his dramatic proclamation of the birth of the People's Republic of China. But even with the tremendous increase in converts during the last few years before the takeover, only 1 percent of the population had been reached for Christianity. What a dismal figure after thirteen centuries of struggle. No wonder Leslie Lyall devoted the eighth chapter of his book, *Red Sky at Night*, to criticism of the missionary movement in China.

Perhaps Mr. Lyall was too hard on himself and the other missionaries. I am confident that those who were called to China were of the same caliber as those sent to India, Africa, and other parts of the globe. No doubt many of them were hard-working, conscientious, dedicated servants of the Lord.

Are you wondering why there wasn't a more impressive figure? Well, there were at least three main obstructions blockading the course of evangelism. In addition to the linguistic and psychological barriers, China simply was not ready religiously. Too many deeply embedded religious philosophies were standing in the way. (In fact, eight hundred deities were accounted for in a 1640 publication.) When the average Chinese was presented with the Gospel of Jesus Christ, his conservative nature, his complacency, and his unwillingness to change his way of life made him throw up his hands and say, "Why should I receive a foreign religion? I have my own."

Because of this philosophy, the average Chinese would rather burn incense than read the Bible. He would prefer to bow before the idols of clay, wood, and stone than worship the true God. Consequently, the few who did accept the Christian way of life were ridiculed by their friends and relatives. They were called traitors, "running dogs for the high nose," and commonly referred to as "foreign religion eaters."

To be fair, those terms were not always misapplied, for there were a number of "rice Christians" who were chiefly interested in the material benefits the missionaries provided. Those pew-warmers never missed the Sunday when canned goods, blankets, soap, towels, and so forth were distributed. Perhaps I would have become a Christian much earlier had I not seen this for myself.

The Dilemma

Obviously, the religious opposition and the weakness within the Church greatly diluted the gospel's effectiveness. No wonder we haven't seen fruit one hundred-fold yet. The problems were too great for the missionaries to handle. In order to weed the garden and fertilize the ground for the greatest harvest, God moved in a dramatic, earthshaking, paradoxical fashion. Let's look at the thrilling way God has been using Chinese Communism to accomplish this great task.

3

The Takeover

. . . how long shall the wicked triumph?

Psalms 94:3

*. . . God is in the heavens: he hath done whatsoever he
hath pleased.*

Psalms 115:3

The nightmare became a reality as the tragic news made
headlines around the world: China has fallen to the Communists! Mao has forced Chiang's government to retreat to Taiwan.

It happened all too quickly!

Mao's army captured Peking in a whirling dust storm on
February 3, 1949. Two months later, when negotiations failed,
the Communists swept across the Yangtze to occupy Nanking.
Then, because the corrupt Kuomintang could hold out no
longer, Shanghai and other cities were taken in the summer.
Before long, Canton, Hainan, and the rest all fell like ripened
apples.

Would the Church fall, too? Was this year to go down in
Christian history as the time God gave up on China?

Obviously an omnipotent God could not be defeated. Nor
would a loving Father turn a deaf ear to the cries of His children. Nevertheless, many fine Christians have written it off as
a bewildering enigma. They feel it's an unsolvable mystery, and
regardless of how grim the facts are, Christians *have* to believe
that God is in control.

Here is good news. There need no longer be a mystery as to
why God allows atheism to rule the mainland. We don't have
to force a belief in God's providence.

Why?

Because the first of five main areas where our Lord has used Communism to accomplish His divine plan is divulged—namely, how God changed the enemy's ingenious organizational plan into a program of blessing and preparation.

Calm in the Storm

In the midst of total confusion, public transportation and postal services ground to a halt, shops closed for fear of looting, and banks shut down because money had lost its value.

However, the Lord of history caused an overall respite among Christians as the Communist propagandists reassured the people they wouldn't interfere with religion. The regime recognized that a significant number of skilled personnel were within the Church. So, to curry their favor and win their confidence, they adopted Article 5 of chapter 1 of the Common Programme on September 29, 1949. This important section of the Chinese People's Political Consultative Conference guaranteed freedom of religious belief.

For the most part, it was "business as usual" in the 11,470 churches, 7,500 gospel centers, 48 seminaries, 21 Bible institutes, 18 Christian universities, 70 Christian hospitals, and by 2,000 ordained Chinese ministers and hundreds of evangelists. Religious broadcasts continued, church services and Bible study groups convened, and seminary graduates marched off to work. In fact, for a short time church attendance actually increased. All in all, there was very little overt interference with religious organizations during the first months of the takeover except the commandeering of church premises in rural areas for the army's use.

One missionary lady was quite optimistic when she arrived in Shanghai from Kaifeng to report that the Communists had not darkened the door of the missionary compound. She was confident that the work could be carried on under the atheistic control. Dr. Andrew Gih, president of the Evangelize China Fellowship, remarked that they still carried on the regular functions in the orphanage for more than a year after the People's Liberation Army came to Shanghai.

Tightening the Grip

The new leaders must have considered religion an important issue because even before the official proclamation of the People's Republic in October, the Religious Advisory Commission was formed. The job of the seven-man committee consisting of five Protestants and two Buddhists was to oversee religious matters. This ecumenical body later gave birth to the two-headed dragon: the Religious Affairs Bureau and the Three-Self Movement. This monster proceeded to devour organized religions and exhale firey persecution in time.

The tough course laid out for Christianity was forecasted by one of the most influential members of the Advisory Commission, the man of the hour, Dr. Y. T. Wu. This liberal minister set the pace for the decade by declaring that since Communism exercises what Christianity professes, Christians all over China should practice what they preach.

On October 1, Mao Tse-tung stood on Tien An-men Square in Peking and announced the birth of the People's Republic of China. On that day he made it crystal clear to the world that the new China was to lean to one side—toward her Big Brother, the Soviet Union (the embodiment of godlessness). He further promised that his government would eliminate bureaucratic and capitalistic classes and reject the West (the sustainer of Christianity in China).

With these opening remarks came new values and new visions which were quickly picked up by the Advisory Commission. This section of their report which came out two months later emphasizes this.

A new chapter in the history of China has begun; a new era has dawned . . . a new philosophy, a new creed and a new mode of living will be instilled into the masses of the people with a vigor that is hitherto scrutinized and, if need be discarded; many new and far-reaching policies will be put into execution. Likewise, much of western culture that has been introduced in recent years will be re-examined and shorn of its undesirable elements. . . . From such a

change there is no turning, and at such a time a diehardness
has no place.[3]

Dr. Wu saw to it that his commission's report was widely
circulated among Christian leaders and mission boards. Then
after the message soaked in for a while, Chou En-lai and other
high Communist officers hosted an historic conference with
several church leaders. The three-day meeting held in Peking
in May 1950 was devised to revolutionize the Church from top
to bottom and force her to march to a different drummer.

Premier Chou began the official rip-off by saying that the
People's Government had no quarrel with the Church as such;
however, he unobtrusively attacked the "imperialistic" foreign
missionaries by accusing them of exploiting religion and poisoning the people's thinking. While admitting their appreciation of
some of the educational and social services of the Church, he
declared that Communists view Christianity as a superstition.
He smilingly affirmed:

> We are going to let you go on teaching, go on trying to
> convert the people; provided you also continue with your
> social services. After all, we both believe that truth will
> prevail; we think your beliefs untrue and false, therefore if
> we are right, the people will reject them, and your church
> will decay. If you are right, then the people will believe
> you; but as we are sure that you are wrong, we are prepared
> for that risk.[4]

In addition, Chou made it clear that if the churches were to
enjoy the constitutional freedom, they must "sweep their
houses clean" and accept the leadership of the Party. To tighten
the grip, he demanded three things:

1.   Policy determination and financial administration must
     be passed over to Chinese leadership.

2.   The missionary's future contribution must lie in special
     service projects only.

3. Mission funds without strings attached would be permitted to enter China temporarily, but from henceforth the Chinese churches would have to be responsible for their own support.

Up to this point, Chinese Christianity always existed on the receiving end. They did the taking and the missionaries did the giving. This was the main attraction for the "rice Christians" we discussed previously. Now suddenly the table was being turned. The Chinese church leaders were being forced to stand on their own two feet. The Communists compelled the Chinese Christians to become independent.

That is precisely what God wanted! The Communists were hoping that by putting the leadership in inexperienced hands and cutting the supply line from the West, they could gain firmer control of the weakened body. But God had other plans. He is the true Sustainer and Controller. He was going to train China's believers to rely on and trust in Him alone. Don't you see how they were playing right into the almighty hand of God? This drastic about-face probably would never have been possible had God not used the atheistic Communists to force the change.

So for the first time in the history of Chinese Christianity the Great Commission was to be placed on the lap of the Chinese alone. With the exception of a few churches which were already independent, it was a radical change.

Wu Wooing

With Chou's inspiration, Y. T. Wu added to his prestige in the Party by drafting the charter of the "new church." His revolutionary Manifesto proclaimed once again that Christianity was a tool of imperialism to exploit the Chinese and warned that the West would try to undermine the New China. Therefore, he called for all Christians to support the Common Political Platform and reform themselves.

Notice this! The Party wanted to use the Manifesto to advocate closer fellowship and unity among the denominations. Isn't it interesting to discover that the modern Western ecumenical movement is not new after all? The Chinese Communist Party fostered it in the early 1950s. Were they trying to strengthen the Church, which they maintained was nothing but superstition? Or were they really making it easier to get a handle on it?

The text of the Manifesto is included for stalwart readers who are courageous enough to attempt reading it.

The Manifesto

Protestant Christianity has been introduced to China for more than a hundred and forty years. During this period it has made a not unworthy contribution to Chinese society. Nevertheless, and this was most unfortunate, not long after Christianity's coming to China, imperialism started its activities here; and since the principal groups of missionaries who brought Christianity to China all came themselves from these imperialistic countries, Christianity consciously or unconsciously, directly or indirectly, became related with imperialism. Now that the Chinese revolution has achieved victory, these imperialistic countries will not rest passively content in face of this unprecedented historical fact in China. They will certainly seek to contrive by every means the destruction of what has actually been achieved; they may also make use of Christianity to forward their plot of stirring up internal dissension, and creating reactionary forces in this country. It is our purpose in publishing the following statement to heighten our vigilance against imperialism, to make the clear political stand of Christians in New China, to hasten the building of a Chinese church whose affairs are managed by the Chinese themselves, and to indicate the responsibilities that should be taken up by Christians throughout the whole country in national reconstruction in New China. We desire to call upon all Christians in the country to exert their best efforts in putting into effect the principles herein presented.

THE TASK IN GENERAL

Christian churches and organizations give thorough-going support to the "Common Political Platform," and under the leadership of the government oppose imperialism, feudalism, and bureaucratic capitalism, and take part in the effort to build an independent, democratic, peaceable, unified, prosperous, and powerful New China.

FUNDAMENTAL AIMS

(1) Christian churches and organizations in China should exert their utmost efforts, and employ effective methods, to make people in the churches everywhere recognize clearly the evils that have been wrought in China by imperialism; recognize the fact that in the past imperialism has made use of Christianity, purge imperalistic influences from within Christianity itself; and be vigilant against imperialism, and especially American imperialism, in its plot to use religion in fostering the growth of reactionary forces. At the same time, the churches and organizations should call upon Christians to participate in the movement opposing war and upholding peace, and teach them thoroughly to understand and support the government's policy of agrarian reform.

(2) Christian churches and organizations in China should take effective measures to cultivate a patriotic and democratic spirit among their adherents in general, as well as a psychology of self-respect and self-reliance. . . . This movement from now onward should complete its tasks within the shortest possible period. At the same time, self-criticism should be advocated, all forms of Christian activity re-examined and re-adjusted, and thoroughgoing austerity measures adopted, so as to achieve the goals of a reformation in the church.

CONCRETE METHODS

(1) All Christian churches and organizations in China that are still relying upon foreign personnel and financial aid should work out concrete plans to realize within the shortest possible time their objective of self-reliance and rejuvenation.

(2) From now onward, as regards their religious work, Christian churches and organizations should lay emphasis upon a deeper understanding of the nature of Christianity itself, closer fellowship and unity among the various denominations, the cultivation of better leadership personnel, and reform in systems of church organization. As regards their more general work, they should emphasize anti-imperialistic, anti-feudalistic and anti-bureaucratic-capitalistic education, together with such forms of service to the people as productive labor, teaching them to understand the New Era, cultural and recreational activities, literacy education, medical and public health work, and care of children.[5]

The Christian community reverberated in protest of Wu's draft; so as a goodwill gesture he made minor changes, and then submitted it again for Chou's approval. It was finally published in July under the title, "Direction of Endeavor for Chinese Christianity in the Construction of New China." (Long titles were very much in vogue so be prepared for them.)

Mission, Impossible

Imagine how the missionaries felt when they saw the signatures of forty church leaders on the document, supposedly indicating it was welcomed by the 400 thousand members they represented! It seemed they were being helplessly dragged into the political arena and would no longer be able to remain aloof.

You may be saying that this is no way to carry out a healthy missionary program. You're absolutely right. It will appear that things are going from bad to worse as you read on.

On April 13, the *People's Daily* carried an article called "How

Imperialism Used Religion for Aggression in China," to accuse churches of having been the bastion of the aggressors for the past 100 years. They built their case around J. Leighton Stuart, former president of a renowned Christian (Yencheng) university, who became the American Ambassador to China. The article claimed he was one of the most important secret agents for American aggression.

Next, the Religious Affairs Bureau got the team together by bringing to Peking 151 Protestant leaders from all over the country for (get ready for another long title) the "Conference on Dealing with Christian Institutions Formerly Receiving American Aid." Then, the Three-Self Movement carried the ball in advocating the Church to become self-governing, self-supporting, and self-propagating.

In this way, the two-headed dragon reared its ugly heads and charged down the field.

It is important to notice here that some missionaries had already been enlightened by God to the benefits of independent churches, but were unable to cut the apron strings. The "clever" Communists did it for them. Although the RAB (Religious Affairs Bureau) intended to uproot Christianity, they were actually only puppets in God's hands.

On the other hand, Communist cadets throughout the land visited the churches and solicited their reactions to the Manifesto. They shoved the document down their throats by asking the reluctant ones why they still welcomed the presence and help of the "imperialist" missionaries.

Consequently, the Western brethren were forced to relinquish their posts, hand over their property deeds, and surrender the control of their educational, medical, and charitable institutions.

Under severe pressure from every side, missionaries found themselves unable to function in any meaningful capacity and decided it was time to leave. (In fact, some had already left.) Before they could get an exit visa though, they needed to secure sponsorship and guarantee for their future conduct from some local people. After taking the lead for so long, it must have been very awkward for them to be put in a subordinate, dependent predicament.

During the first year of the Three-Anti and Five-Anti campaigns (attempts to get rid of the old system), the China Inland Mission, which was established in 1865 by Hudson Taylor, ordered a massive withdrawal. The complete evacuation included 601 adults and their 284 children.

As other mission boards followed suit, government officials invited the Catholic leaders to exchange views on the Catholic Church Reform Movement. At that meeting, the vice-chairman Lu Ting-yi urged Catholics all over China to unite and sever all relationships with imperialism. Chou En-lai emphasized that guests should not be present when the house is being cleaned. Then he added this:

> The Reform Movement initiated by the religious circles should be promoted. The People's Government will give it aid and support. This is a patriotic movement of the religious circles. To love one's fatherland is the duty of all, including Catholics.[6]

Shortly after, many Catholic clergymen united with the Party line and patterned themselves after the Three-Self Movement. It then became evident that the Catholics would not escape the pruning saws. So two thousand of their missionaries packed up and slipped out as the Bamboo Curtain began to close.

Sharpening the Picture

It doesn't take a genius to tell what's been happening. The Communists' complaint against the Church has been its "imperialistic" ties. Now that they have successfully eliminated the missionaries under the banner of "anti-imperialism," they should be satisfied.

Not on your life!

So far they have been whacking away the branches. From now on, they are going to chop at the roots until the tree finally falls. Yes, the organized Church will be destroyed.

If you are feeling depressed, forget it; because before this organized Church is cut down, God will pick the fruits; and from them seeds will sprout. This underground Church ". . . shall be like a tree planted by the rivers of water, that bringeth forth his fruit in his season; his leaf also shall not wither; and whatsoever he doeth shall prosper" (Psalms 1:3).

Guidance and Control

Now that the leadership of the Church had been forced into less-experienced hands, the Party took advantage of the situation and began to guide and train them onto the socialistic path.

Peking summoned 232 Protestant delegates from 62 different organizations for the First National Christian Conference from July 22 to August 15, 1954. From this came the new 139-member New National Committee whose purpose was to guide the movement of independence in administration, support, and propagation of the church in China.

The Committee drafted a message of "respect" to Chairman Mao saying they had successfully freed themselves from the influences of imperialism. It gave Mao all the credit by stating:

> . . . All these successes are inseparable from your wise leadership and deep concern as well as the brilliant achievements of New China for the past several years. We are, therefore, offering our deepest gratitude on behalf of the entire Christians![7]

Under the guise of "loving the country and the church," the New National Committee urged the Christian community to learn patriotism seriously and take down denominational fences. It became mandatory for all churches to fly the red five-star flag.

Pastoral Indoctrination

In order to further mold the Church into the shape they wanted and to gradually shift her allegiance from God to Communism, they began a training program for church leaders.

The three-month-long indoctrination classes for preachers

began with the first five-year plan. In Shanghai, for example, the authorities used systematic methods including weekly discussions and lectures to train the fifty-three ordained pastors in Communist theory. The RAB appointed nine Party members as instructors along with some "progressive" Christian leaders.

After beginning the day with a token half-hour devotional period, the rest of the time was spent in listening to lectures and participating in secular discussions. To sprinkle a little "divine salt" on the proceedings, choral contributions were added.

Here is a thumbnail sketch of what was covered:

1. Purpose and correct attitude toward the study class.

2. The greatness and loveliness of the country through comparison of the old and new China.

3. The nature of imperialism and how it used the churches to accomplish its goals.

4. The meaning of the Three-Self Movement and the religious policy of the government.

At the conclusion of the seminars, the pastors were ordered to compose personal, autobiographical review essays.

Can you guess what they were trying to do? They wanted to reveal the student's past life to see how he identified with the purpose and plans of new China.

An example can be seen in Y. T. Wu's article on "How the Communist Party Has Educated Me." Wu began his autobiography by reviewing his past and then proceeded with the following points:

1. [Communism] has taught me the true meaning of the verse, "Love your enemies."

2. The Communist party helped me to recognize the true face of imperialism, and to see the most pressing problem today for China, as indeed for the whole world, is how to destroy imperialism and set up peoples' governments.

3. The Communist party enabled me to understand the true meaning of revolution.

4. The Communist party made me understand the true position of the proletariat.

5. The Communist party has shown me the true relation between theory and practice, between faith and deeds.[8]

Doctrine in the Blender

It was not enough just to indoctrinate the pastors; they must succeed in diluting the doctrines of the Bible with Marxist-Leninist ideology before they could use the pulpits as soapboxes to spout out their dogmas.

How could they possibly mix atheism with Christianity? It would be a pretty crafty trick, wouldn't it? This is how they set out to accomplish this feat.

The RAB State Council director declared during the Second National Conference on Religious Work in Peking that positive values of patriotism should take the place of negative religious propaganda.

While he admitted the Communists can accept certain parts of the Bible as reasonable, he insisted that it was necessary to infuse the Christian doctrine with Marxist-Leninist thought.

His finale was to point out that the real purpose of the Bible was to advocate peace and philanthropy without class distinction. The director gave his official approval to the Ten Commandments but dismissed the supernatural records, the Second Coming of Christ, and the end of the world as fables. (Sounds familiar, doesn't it?)

Sermon Censorship

Apparently these preceding programs weren't entirely successful. Why else would they have to resort to sermon censorship? The clergy was officially ordered to conform to the directives in the Party's new stand on religion. To achieve the

maximum effect, numerous articles were circulated ordering
pastors and priests to submit drafts of their sermons for censorship.

The clergymen were in no position to argue; for the RAB had
them over a barrel. For some time they had begun compiling
a secret dossier on every clergyman or administrative religious
worker. The files included photographs, biographies, up-to-date
records of political activities, samples of handwriting, and remarks made in the sermons. (One thing you have to give them
credit for—they're thorough!)

Preachers who emphasized the conflicts between religion
and the world system, or contained thoughts of dying for one's
religion, were singled out and called before the RAB to be
"persuaded and educated." Their personal file swelled with
each such visit.

Wolves in Sheep's Clothing

The Lord warns in Matthew 13:25 that Satan sows tares
among the wheat. I wonder if the Communists weren't inspired
by this verse for this next move.

The Communists sent previous members and clergy who
were "converted" to the Party line back to their churches as
spies. These "hidden strength" operators were instructed to
openly oppose preachers who delivered supernatural-type sermons.

Along with this diabolical practice, there was also the "single
string connections" whose job was to secularize the churches.
They were to collect information, "convert" believers, gradually take over the organization, replace the leaders, and instill
fear among the congregation.

Subsequently, true believers began to feel out of place in the
church and began holding their own private meetings.

Dumping Rome

To gain even greater organizational control over the Catholic
Church, several conferences were held. They were aimed at

eliminating their strong tie with the Vatican. The National Conference of Catholics and the Congress of Catholics and others resulted in the formation of the Independent National Catholic Church. This was a progressive, patriotic organization.

Under the auspices of the National Catholic Patriotic Association, ties were officially broken with the Pope. The Chinese leaders ignored the April, 1951 decree prohibiting unapproved consecration, and consecrated two bishops in Wuhan. Although it meant automatic excommunication, they proceeded with similar ceremonies in six additional areas.

Independence from Rome at last!

Ecumenical Invasion

The Party wasn't yet satisfied with the church they had molded. More drastic measures were in the works. Up until now they managed to at least superficially respect Article 88 of the new 1954 constitution which specified that: "Every citizen of the People's Republic of China shall have freedom of religious belief." Except for scattered incidents in rural areas, outright prohibition and utter overt despotism were reserved.

But now the scene begins to change. Under the pretense of "church unification," all church property and programs were surrendered to the Three-Self Movement's local committee. (Why does the same group that advocated self-reliance demand that they be governed?)

This committee was to approve of everything: the worship program, the selection and editing of acceptable hymns, the screening of commentaries, and so forth. Because the churches had no option but to follow the dictatorship thrust upon them, they had to abide by articles of union such as this one for the city of Taiyuan: (This is very important.)

There shall be unified worship for the city of Taiyuan, and a ministerial staff of three or four. All fellow workers besides these, and those assigned to the Three Self office, shall throw themselves into the socialist construction of our mother country. Those who are older or physically weak shall retire. All real and movable church property and all church funds shall be turned over to the Three Self Committee.

Church Organization

1. All former governing committees and boards of the various churches are hereby abolished, and the administration of the church shall be in the hands of the Three Self Committee.

2. Regarding ritual, regulations, and church order:

a. There shall be a unified worship program, and each church shall surrender its own individual ritual.

b. The hymns used in worship shall be unified, and a committee shall choose and edit the hymns for use.

c. All books used in the interpretation of the Bible shall be examined and judged, and those containing poisonous thoughts shall be rejected. Only teachings favoring union and socialism shall be used. In particular, any material coming from outside [probably referring to material sent in by mail from Hong Kong] shall be carefully examined before being accepted.

d. There shall be no more preaching about the Last Day, or about the vanity of this world. This is negative and pessimistic teaching. Instead we shall emphasize the need for the union of faith and practice, the dignity of labor, the control of nature, and the dividing line between ourselves and our enemies, between right and wrong.

e. Belief and unbelief shall not be made an issue in determining the marriage questions.

3. In regard to the necessary reform of each church:

a. The Little Flock shall abolish its women's meetings, its weekly breaking of bread, its personal interviews with members before the breaking of bread, and its rule against women speaking in the church.

b. The Salvation Army shall give up all its military regulations.

c. The Seventh-day Adventists shall abolish their daily morning prayers. On the Sabbath day they shall participate in beneficial good works and in economic production. Their tithe system for the support of the clergy shall be abolished, and also their unification of accounts for Shansi Province.

d. All the Y.M.C.A. secretaries shall be assigned to productive labor, and the closing of the Taiyuan Y.M.C.A. as a separate organization shall be carefully considered.[9]

Closed Churches—Opened Homes

It is not difficult to imagine what happened next, is it? The 200 churches in Shanghai were reduced to 23. Peking had only 4 churches open rather than 65 as in years past. The zealous Communists (under the banner of the Three-Self Movement) went on to dissolve the Jesus Family communities and took over (or closed) 3 Catholic universities, 189 secondary schools, 2,011 primary schools, and 2,243 prayer schools—involving 30,000 students in all. The Union Theological Seminary in Canton was also closed down due to "a shortage of personnel."

Some have estimated that by 1959 approximately 80 percent of the churches in China were closed. Now the big question is, What happened to all the Christians?

Well, if you were a born-again believer living in China, what would you do? Keep in mind that the preacher is a Party "convert" who delivers a censored sermon, picks out only approved and edited hymns for the ecumenically minded service, and preaches to a dwindling congregation sprinkled with spies. How would you respond? Would you continue to attend the "services" or would you strike out on your own to worship and fellowship elsewhere?

Secret home meetings sprang up more and more.

The wife of a former professor at Peking University gave a testimony when she escaped from Shanghai to Hong Kong. She said there were many small groups formed by people whose churches had been closed down or taken over. They met irregularly but frequently at different homes for Bible studies and

prayer meetings and were filling a tremendous spiritual
vacuum which the Communist Party created. She testified that
many souls were being saved through these little meetings and
that people risked persecution, imprisonment, and counter-
revolutionary charges in attending them.

A Hong Kong newspaper added credence to her testimony
in its article on the underground church:

> As services had become so formal and so preoccupied
> with Marxist-Leninist propaganda, Christians were *meet-
> ing in private small house groups,* even at the risk of arrest
> for breaking the law forbidding private assembly.[10]

A Look in the Rearview Mirror

As time sped through the course of history, we saw how God
successfully divided the sheep from the goats.

The Church as an organization has been sifted through the
stages of confusion, isolation, fragmentation, condemnation, op-
pression, and nationalization. Finally it became a political pulpit, an arm of Communistic propaganda. Truth ceased to be
absolute and became a servant of the state. The bond of Christian love was replaced by militancy. And the organized
churches were "united."

We have seen all this happen step by step.

On October 10, 1959, *Heavenly Wind* [*Tien Feng*] *Magazine,*
the only religious publication in China, printed an article called
"Ten Years of Struggle in Opposing Imperialism and Loving
Our Country." It described the former Church as a tool for
missionaries' private and imperialistic purposes. Then it went
on to praise the effectiveness of the socialistic educational
movement in remodeling the thinking of the Christians.

Six Australian churchmen who toured China reported that all
branches of the Christian Church had been brought into line
and there was absolute unity among the churches.

After a decade of religious coercion, the urge to celebrate was
too strong for the Party and the Religious Affairs Bureau to
resist. Ignoring stark failures in many of the Party's best laid

plans (like the Great Leap Forward, for example), they put on their best clothes and paraded the new church up and down the streets. They wanted China's teeming millions to rejoice with them in bidding good riddance to "naked imperialist aggression," "imperialist use of missionary work," and "Bible-reading wolves."

Now they were pulling the strings to make it dance to their tune and they wanted to gloat publicly in their success.

This carcass of the old Church was dragged through the crowded streets and applauded as having reached "maturity" under the glorious guidance of the Party.

Have you ever wondered how Job's enemies acted after God took away the hedge and allowed Satan to rob Job of his financial resources and relatives? Do you suppose they rejoiced because Job got his "just deserts?" I think they did.

Here at this moment in history the true believer could really identify with him. The Church's financial resources were cut off; the believer's spiritual relatives were alienated.

What next?

Read Job 2:5, 6. You will find out what the following chapter is all about:

> But put forth thine hand now, and touch his bone and his flesh, and he will curse thee to thy face.
>
> And the Lord said unto Satan, Behold, he is in thine hand; but save his life.

4

The Gates of Hell

*And I will turn my hand upon thee, and purely purge
away thy dross, and take away all thy tin. . . .*

Isaiah 1:25

*Take away the dross from the silver, and there shall come
forth a vessel for the finer.*

Proverbs 25:4

In his report to the Committee on the Judiciary of the United
States Senate in July, 1971, Richard L. Walker stated that the
human cost of Communism in China had reached somewhere
between 34,300,000 to 63,784,000 lives.[11]

By comparison, Mao makes Hitler look like a little schoolboy.

An escapee to Hong Kong related this grisly account of mass
murder:

I was conscripted by the Communists to drive one of
their death trucks. I did not drive in the daytime, but by
night. By far the greater number of executions were done
secretly, and after dark. The victims were tied up hands
and feet and loaded into our trucks like logs—120 of them
to a truck. All night long I drove back and forth from the
prisons to the river banks. The authorities didn't even
bother with wasting shot on the victims. They were simply
dumped into the river and drowned. I could not stand this
nefarious traffic nor bear to hear the screams and moans of
the helpless prisoners—so one day I jumped from the truck
and fled.[12]

This private "war" was aimed at eliminating landlords, bureaucrats, capitalists, reactionaries, and antirevolutionary elements. Although many Christians must have been included in the carnage after the takeover, the actual onslaught against the Church was yet in the making.

A Satanic Scheme

At a secret meeting of the RAB in Peking, methods of dealing with the religious community were discussed. An important official from the Party's propaganda department pointed out that since religion was a form of social consciousness, total forbiddance would only hurt the Party. Prohibition by administrative orders would result in fanaticism and maybe religious riots. His punch line was, "If we are to destroy it, we must do it gradually by other methods."

Battle for the Mind

One of the first tactics used against those under the banner of Jesus Christ was the Learning Meetings. Christians were herded into month-long "recording sessions" all over the country where they were instructed to respond to the RAB reports on current political and economic events, both domestic and foreign. Most important of all, they were to be enlightened on the regime's policy toward religion and past imperialistic aggression.

Just listening to reports and writing an agreeable commentary wouldn't be so bad. The anguish lay in the fact that they were forced into six-member groups and required to come up with personal experiences to support what was talked about. Furthermore, all that took place was recorded and kept on file with the community leader.

For those who tried to avoid this painful procedure or had trouble getting rid of their "poisonous imperialistic thinking" after attending the meetings, their neighbors and relatives would be called upon to publicly expose them.

If one remained in his stubborn condition, then more drastic "assistance" was given—separation from family, friends, relatives, and the outside world for the "group therapy" stage. This created feelings of uncertainty and disorientation along with physical and mental fatigue.

The tremendous pressure broke many down and forced them to write autobiographies in minute detail. This was similar to the assignment given pastors previously. These life stories were to begin with earliest recollections at around seven years of age and were supposed to include the innermost thoughts of the individual.

Accusers of the Brethren

The Three-Self Movement leaders recognized that many had failed to progress in their thinking as was hoped, so another plan was put into effect.

Receptacles were placed around the city or village to invite the public to report those who were not conforming to the Party line. This way the government would be anonymously informed of any suspicious elements. This witch-hunt led to the arrest of hundreds of thousands of people who faced a public trial called an Accusation Meeting, or immediate execution.

Often the Party would choose to make a public example of a Christian, and especially a pastor, who refused to swallow the new rationale at the expense of his own beliefs. To publicly denounce a church leader would be a strong blow against the body of Christ, so it became a favorite weapon.

On one such occasion, 25 hundred prominent ministers were ordered to attend as witnesses of the proceedings; perhaps they were being warned of what could happen to them.

To give you an idea of what happened during an Accusation Meeting, here is a suggested agenda taken from a fellow named Liu Liang-mo who wrote a pamphlet on "How to Hold a Successful Accusation Meeting."

1. Speeches containing derogatory remarks about the accused given by his closest friends and associates.
2. A list of accusations.

3. Demand for government to mete out punishment.
4. Personal confession from the accused.

These meetings were well planned and skillfully coordinated to incite the crowd into an angry mob. Speakers would often use violent language to accuse their victims in the name of patriotism. Here is an example taken from Bishop Kaung's speech:

> Today I arise with extreme indignation and shame to denounce that Christian reprobate W. Y. Ch'en, who, hidden within the Methodist Church, has been a willing tool of American imperialism and bandit Chiang Kai-shek and has worked against the people and against the revolution.

To justify these harsh words against his friend and brother bishop, he listed three particulars and finally thanked the Communists for arresting Bishop Chen. After asking that they punish him severely according to the law, he concluded with this confession:

> I must also make a deep criticism of myself. . . . I am determined to put public duty above private feelings in reorganizing our church, and will cleanse the church of all reprobates like W. Y. Ch'en, whether they be few or many. . . .[13]

One after another, faithful servants of the Lord were raked over the coals in the name of anti-imperialism. To add insult to injury, the Party held up Jesus Christ as an example by saying that He accused the Pharisees.

The "religious" press also supported the campaign with enthusiasm. It carried detailed reports of the meetings and a list of each victim's crimes.

Self-Criticism

If the authorities couldn't find anyone to criticize you in one of their Accusation Meetings, they would insist that you do a job on yourself. Sometimes, a fellow like Bishop Kaung who had surrendered his Christian faith, would happily participate in self-criticism to gain the Party's favor. He welcomed the opportunity to show his progressiveness in changing his thinking.

Revival Meetings

As an additional wedge to pry the Church away from its moorings, the RAB borrowed from the Church the concept of "revival meetings."

All over China they called doubters and "sinners" to repent, confess, and see the light of the Communist gospel. They insisted that all Christians turn over a new leaf, to conform to the new society, to accomplish new goals and a new life-style.

Meanwhile Back at Headquarters. . . .

The Party leaders were dissatisfied with the sluggish progress on the religious front. The RAB was criticized for being complacent because their achievements could not compare with advancements in other fields. The clarion call to take more drastic measures was sounded.

Preachers in a Pickle

The new "get tough" policy began with the pastors at large. They were considered parasites of society and their work was labeled nonproductive. Under the slogan, "No preacher should live at the expense of others," they were forced into the production line.

Some were sent for full-time factory work while others were forced to band together to initiate their own productive activities. For example, in Kweilin (capital of Kwangsi Province), Protestant and Catholic clergy established the Red Light Pickle Factory. Others fared no better—they could be found licking envelopes, digging ditches, or fertilizing the fields.

Rectification Arrests

As the antirightest campaign waged on, those who refused to conform or failed to satisfy the government's demands for change were loaded into paddy wagons by the hundreds and hauled away for incarceration.

So much for religious freedom!

Arrests were made in homes and streets at any time, day or night, often without a formal charge. Frequently Christians were booked on the pretext of having committed crimes against the people.

Sisters of the Sacred Heart Home for Children in Nanking were accused of deliberately starving, neglecting, torturing, and selling Chinese children.

Something unusual happened one night when the police raided the homes of six priests, several pastors, and Jesuit fathers in Shanghai. After several of the Jesuits were taken to jail, the others were put under house arrest.

News of this violation of religious freedom soon spread, and thousands of Catholics gathered at the square of Siccawei. They knelt to say the rosary opposite the house where the priests were under Communist guard. In spite of the machine guns pointed at them, more and more Catholics gathered. Their voices reciting the rosary louder and louder in unison with prayers for the imprisoned priests made a magnificent scene.

Life Behind Bars?

The massive arrests resulted in such severe overcrowding in the prisons that the inmates couldn't even lie down and had to take turns sleeping. (Of course there was no protesting privilege!) In these cells, which were like ice in the winter and ovens in the summer, the prisoners had to sit motionless on the ground from dawn to dusk. Any attempt to close their eyes during this period of time would bring an angry roar from the guard.

The monotony of this routine was only interrupted by interrogations. The prisoner was brought face to face with his malignant judge who sought to trap him with every question. Without counsel and forbidden to take notes on his replies or details of the questions, he had only his memory to help him recall what had been said. If his responses were considered insufficient or insolent, or if he refused to speak altogether, he was kept standing at attention for hours or days. Chains and manacles were loaded on his hands and feet. Thus pinioned to the walls of his cell like an animal, he had to remain until he begged for mercy and consented to cooperate.

Another favorite technique was the Pavlovian system which uses the alternation of cold and heat, light and darkness, and talking sessions with solitary confinement. Orders against sleep and the effect of one-hour-long days or thirty-six-hour-long nights often brought about a complete removal of suppressed desires.

Continuous brainwashing through various techniques often produces a stage of complete nervous collapse. According to reliable sources, a person who is subjected to this kind of treatment would have dilated pupils, quick and shallow breathing, rigid body, and perspiring skin. He would often become hysterical and lose control. Recovery to normalcy would take months, if not years.[14]

God allowed the purifying fire to touch His children because He was interested in building a powerful army for His future program. Needless to say, many failed to pass the tests.

M. E. Loewen, a Seventh-Day Adventist missionary to China and now an associate editor of *Liberty* magazine, declared in that publication: "I know . . . that within a few years of the communist takeover in 1949, nearly three out of four of all professed Christians abandoned ship. . . . Hundreds of thousands of Christians vanished. Most are presumed dead. The survivors are underground."

The Price of Purity

The heros of faith who entered the fiery furnace because they refused to deny the Lord have certainly paid a dear price. But Matthew 5:10–12 promises great reward:

Blessed are they which are persecuted for righteousness' sake: for their's is the kingdom of heaven.

Blessed are ye, when men shall revile you, and persecute you, and shall say all manner of evil against you falsely, for my sake.

Rejoice, and be exceeding glad: for great is your reward in heaven: for so persecuted they the prophets which were before you.

The alarming fate of some prominent pastors and churches have reached the West in spite of the Bamboo Curtain. As their story unfolds in these next few pages, you will be impressed once more that while salvation is free, it is not cheap!

Nee and the Flock

Watchman Nee, who founded the prolific Little Flock, was arrested in April of 1952. This noted author and pastor was charged with the crime of being a capitalist and accused of five other transgressions, including multiple adultery for seducing over one hundred women.

Without a trial he was sentenced to fifteen years in prison.

A campaign against the Little Flock spread from Shanghai to many other cities. Their leaders were charged with carrying on destructive activities, breaking down government policies and control movements, spreading reactionary ideas and counter-revolutionary rumors, instilling fear in the hearts of church members, poisoning the minds of youth, and destroying church unity.

After four years of re-education, the character of the Little Flock movement changed considerably. This "reformed Christian assembly" was then permitted to join the Three-Self Movement.

Although Nee was supposed to be freed in 1969, the World Vision Asian News Report stated that he was not fully released, but rather transferred to a Shanghai prison. There he was to continue in the translation of technical books from English into Chinese for the government. It further said that he received a small salary for his work and was allowed to go home once or twice a month.

In February of 1972 a letter arrived in Hong Kong saying that Nee was transferred again, this time to a camp some distance from Shanghai. When his wife died, he not only suffered deep sorrow, but was stripped of his only privilege—his visits home.

Ching and the Family

The indigenous Jesus Family was dealt with in 1952 also. The leader, Ching Tien-ying, was arrested and charged with being a dictator and adulterer. In a seemingly contradictory move, the Party disbanded the Family's communes and eliminated their cooperative working spirit. It seems that in a Communist country there is no coexistence of similar systems.

In his book, *The Jesus Family in Communist China,* Dr. Rees testifies that during the first months of the takeover, Party officers would show amazement at the tremendous efficiency and sacrificial cooperative working spirit of the Ye-Su Chia-ting (Jesus Family) in Ma Chuang. He recalls incidents of Communist leaders visiting the "Family" and wanting to know how they prevented people from stealing the grapes and how they stopped nurses from stealing drugs.

One Communist officer asked, "How do you make the nurses take an interest in their work and love the children?" The answer was, "If they have the Lord Jesus in their hearts then all the questions are solved."

The apparent success of the Jesus Family system caused the envy and animosity of the Party toward them. They could not escape eventual persecution because they had put into practice a Marxist-Leninist ideal in a far superior way.

Wei and the Church

Like the Jesus Family, the True Jesus Church was also purely Chinese. That is, it was independent of missionary support and control. Do you suppose the Party could find fault with it for being "imperialistic"? Isaac Wei's self-examination below will give you the answer and probably raise some new questions, such as "What really happened at the summer study institute in Peking?"

My Self-Examination

I used to think that since our church has had no relations with American imperialism and has never been supported financially by reactionaries or bureaucrats, it would be hard to find anything in the church to denounce. . . . But after the summer study institute in Peking the eyes of my heart have been enlightened so that I have now honestly and deeply realized that I myself have been pro-American and against Soviet Russia, the Party and the People. . . . I wish to admit frankly and without regard to face that the Three-Self church which I preached was not thoroughgoing, it was only an unconscious tool of imperialism, feudalism and bureaucratic capitalism.

For example, my teaching of being above politics, above country, above the world and above class was just the result of imperialist poisonous thinking; yet I complacently thought that this was true spirituality. . . .

Our self-support idea was also inadequate. Although it is true that we did not use the financial support of imperialism and reactionary governments, still our country churches depended to a great extent on the financial support of feudalistic landlords, and to tell the truth I had never denounced feudalism. Also our preachers were all taken out of production, we had not followed Paul in laboring day and night to support ourselves, and so in many places our church, after the land reform, faded away, because our method of self-support had been to depend on the landlords. . . .

In self-government our record is still more shameful. Although we had denounced the greed and corruption of the old society, still our church welcomed the bureaucrats and capitalists of the cities. . . . We often elected bureaucrats and capitalists to responsible positions in the church . . . anyone with money and influence, if he only showed a little piety, would be sure to be elected, and there were even some who did not truly love the Lord who got elected. . . .[15]

Wang Ming-tao

There were other pastors, such as Wang Ming-tao, who insisted on exercising their freedom of religious rights and refused to conform or go underground. In spite of mounting pressure, Wang fearlessly thundered out his opposition to the liberal government-controlled Three-Self Movement. He insisted that the Church could never come to terms with the world and continued with the theme of "Love Not the World." Time and again he employed his faultless Mandarin to eloquently defend the purity of the Faith from his pulpit in the Christian Tabernacle.

This spiritual warrior who once bought a coffin and kept it in his house to show his willingness to die for the Faith, was finally ordered to attend his Accusation Meeting.

In front of delegates ordered to come from churches and Christian organizations all over Peking, Reverend Wang was charged with three crimes:

1. He was not sympathetic with the government.
2. He refused to take part in the Three-Self Movement.
3. His preaching was individualistic and its purpose unclear.

As Wang sat quietly on the makeshift platform with his eyes fixed upward, one after another rose up to denounce him. Amid the excitement some sat silently, some wept, while others tried to leave as a protest. Although the presiding officials used their favorite techniques to condemn him to death, only about one-fourth of those present agreed that he should even be imprisoned.

The meeting finally broke up without reaching any conclusion except to suspend Wang's preaching privileges. He breathed a sigh of relief in earning a stay of execution at least for the time being.

A few days later some students in Peking organized an "Oppose the Persecution of Wang Ming-tao" campaign which was publicized all over China.

With his preaching privilege suspended, Wang continued his ministry through the written word. Since printers were afraid to accept his business, he proceeded to set up his own type and printing facilities. He authored many books and pamphlets and wrote for his own *Spiritual Food Quarterly* magazine.

He published a powerful indictment of the Three-Self Movement entitled "Betraying the Son of Man with a Kiss," and distributed a forceful pamphlet called "We Because of Our Faith" to his congregation.

It stated in part:

> . . . We will not be united with unbelievers, and we will never join any of their organizations. . . . We shall make whatever sacrifice is required of us in being faithful to God. The twisting of the Word and the consequent falsehoods cannot intimidate us.

Wang maintained that he was neither pro-Western nor narrowly chauvinistic; he was only deeply committed to truth and integrity. He accused the Three-Self Movement of not being explicit and truthful about his alleged "poisonous activities." He continued to say:

> In conclusion, a word to the saints. In the Scriptures there is nothing but the pure truth of God, without any "imperialistic poison." . . . We must go on believing and preaching it. Nobody can interfere with us, and nobody can forbid us to do this. We are ready to pay any price to preserve the Word of God and we are equally willing to sacrifice anything in order to preach the Word of God. . . . Dear brothers and sisters, let us be strong through the mighty power of the Lord! Let us profess our faith with courage and spread the Gospel with zeal! Let us be pre-

pared to be faithful to the Lord at any cost! Our God is almighty and He will keep all those who are faithful to Him. Our Lord is the Lord of victory, who will lead us from victory unto victory. Now is the time for us to stand up and fight for His holy name, for His Gospel and for His church. Don't be cowards! Don't be weary! Don't give way! Don't compromise! The battle is indeed furious and the battlefield certainly full of dangers, but God's glory will be manifest there. He will honor them who honor Him. He will glorify those who glorify Him. Hark! The trumpet has been blown! Look, the victory is in sight! My dear brothers and sisters, let us follow in the steps of the Lord and, holding aloft His banner, go forward courageously for His Gospel's sake.[16]

It seemed for a moment that Truth had prevailed and Wang Ming-tao would be able to continue as a gallant soldier of the cross. Attendance at Wang's church increased along with a tremendous rise in membership.

Riding on the tide of his victory, Wang began to preach to the largest crowds ever in January. In spite of the bitter cold, hundreds of people stood outside the church building listening from the loud speakers and many of them were saved.

Being unable to take him by force due to public support, the Three-Self Movement leaders decided to make a final attempt to win him over. A committee of six prominent leaders of the movement showed up at Pastor Wang's front door and requested to speak with him. Wang's refusal humiliated them and they began publishing lists of accusations in the *Heavenly Wind* magazine to denounce him throughout the country. Among other things, he was accused of being unpatriotic and having no feeling for the people.

On July 25 a special denunciation meeting was held in Hankow with forty-nine men appointed as Wang's accusers. Fervent denunciations were addressed to the crowd picturing Wang as a dangerous enemy of the Church and of the nation. All the skills in holding such meetings were utilized to whip the crowd into a fervor of indignation. However, his enemies were no more successful than before and the meeting ended haphazardly.

During this time, Wang held two weeks of special meetings which, as previously, were packed to capacity. On August 7 he continued his theme of Jesus' betrayal and preached another sermon entitled "They in This Manner Betrayed Jesus." Afterwards, he again passed out his powerful pamphlet "We Because of Our Faith."

Early next morning, August 8, the Communists felt they could wait no longer in laying their hands on their most outspoken and popular critic. Wang and his wife were awakened, tied up, and taken off to be arrested and charged with resisting the government. He was sentenced without a trial to fifteen years in prison.

Upon his arrival at the prison, Wang was put in the hands of two Communist agents who constantly debated and argued with him. After a year's constant hounding and brainwashing, this psychological warfare broke him down both physically and mentally. He was quite literally beside himself, for it was reported that he would pace around yelling, "I am Peter!" and then later scream, "I am Judas!"

Under these physical circumstances he signed what was called a "confession" and submitted it for reformation. His self-examination paper was read at a public meeting:

> I am a counterrevolutionary offender. . . . As a result of the patient attitude shown by the government and the re-education given me I have come to realize my errors. I have been accorded generous treatment by the government and have been saved from the abyss of crime. For this my heart is full of gratitude.[17]

As a result of Wang's physical and mental breakdown, his prison sentence was shortened to just thirteen months. He was released on September 30, 1956.

Later on when his health improved, he and his wife repudiated the confession. They said it did not contain his true convictions and was not in his own words. So he was imprisoned again and subjected to similar treatment, this time on a lifetime sentence. After serving twelve years in a Peking jail, the sixty-eight-year-old pastor was moved to a labor camp in northern Shansi, in 1968.

War on Religion

The explosion of China's first atom bomb in Sinkiang was an ominous warning of things to come. . . .

After closing 90 percent of the churches and silencing the most powerful and eloquent foes of the RAB, the press launched a full-scale attack against all religions. This included Buddhism, Taoism, ancestor worship, and all other forms of worship of any deity.

Religion was blamed for sluggishness in political reform. The Party's publication, *Red Flag*, bluntly declared: "Religion is our enemy. Religion is guilty. Form a united front against religion." The phony front of religious tolerance was completely torn down. Even the official churches were in disrepute.

Scores of articles appeared in both religious and secular presses debating the pros and cons of wiping out all religions. All forms of religion and superstitions were lumped into one category and denounced as backward and counterrevolutionary.

Satan was getting ready to launch a full-scale war against the body of Christ who were now worshiping in the underground cell groups. Because the believers clung to their Saviour, their faith would be tested, like Job's was, as the prince of this world unleashed all his fury.

The Cultural Revolution

At this decisive point in time, seventy-three-year-old Mao brooded in his secluded residence on the eastern hills of Peking. He was desperately plotting a course toward reviving his waning influence in China.

Finally he decided to bypass the normal procedure and summoned a secret session of the Central Committee. Ad hoc committees were quickly set up as the midwife to handle the labor in giving birth to Mao's brainchild—the Cultural Revolution. Little did he know that this desperate fling was to result in an unprecedented turbulence since the dawn of China's civilization.

The preparation for the birth of Mao's baby included a massive Communistic evangelism program designed to touch the very souls of the people. More than 12 thousand mobile teams equipped with projectors, generators, and screens traveled from village to village to prepare the ground.

As the Maoists devised to harness the strength of the impressionable youth to stem the tide of intellectual revisionism, the old-line conservative officers were fighting hard against radicalization in domestic policy. The battle of words raged high. Maoists and Liuists openly carried out the duel.

The struggle and pain within the Party finally produced a child. The first Red Guard group was approved thirteen days after the Central Committee meeting on May 16.

The newly formed Red Guards of the Tsinghua University were soon followed by many others and the first "big character" posters appeared on the walls of Peking on June 1. Only two days later 160 prominent members of the Peking Party Committee were purged.

Thus the Cultural Revolution, the children's nightmare began its full swing.

Hell's Angels

With the roaring of the first volley of guns in Peking came the announcement that all universities and high schools were to be closed for six months. These revolutionary-minded youth would soon become Mao's little generals in the violent campaign against the "four olds"—old thoughts, old habits, old cultures, and old customs.

After being provided with free transportation and lodging, and in many cases free food and clothing, millions of them would become drunk with power as they wasted cities and villages throughout the mainland.

The Famous Swim

In spite of his deteriorating health, Mao attempted to revive the spirit of his famous Long March of the mid-30s by baptizing his seventy-three-year-old body in the Yangtze River in Hankow on July 16. The desperate leader took his dramatic swim to disprove rumors of his ill health or even death. Photographs showing him in the muddy torrent with his admirers appeared in newspapers and magazines around the world. Mao had successfully proved that he was both willing and able to lead China's masses through his Great Proletarian Cultural Revolution.

Hang God

Suddenly tons of paper and torrents of ink were used in public display. Large posters saying, HANG GOD appeared everywhere.

Violent attacks broke out in many cities in the craze to eliminate the "relic of the feudal past." Not only were Christians at large and adherents of various religions potential victims, even the turncoat Three-Self Movement leaders would not escape the fury of the fire.

Church leaders in Canton, Swatow, and Shanghai were forced to sit or kneel in the gutters to be mocked and spat upon. Others had their hair shaved in the shape of a cross as a heinous brand while some were paraded through the streets as religious "bad elements." Often they would be required to wear placards saying, "I am a liar and deceiver," and repeat the words at intervals before the jeering mobs.

An eighty-year-old Christian lady's house was ransacked and her Bibles torn to pieces. While being taunted to confess there was no God, she replied, "How can I? I have believed in Him for forty years."

An elderly pastor was forced by the Red Guards in Shanghai to bow before the portrait of Chairman Mao in spite of his firm refusal. The young hoodlums kicked, beat, and pushed him down before the picture of China's new god. Bruised and bleeding, he was led through the city wearing a dunce cap, and then taken into prison never to be seen again.

In Canton an elderly woman discovered by Red Guards in possession of a Bible was stripped, smeared with honey, and made to stand in the hot sun for many hours.

A young man was tugged through the streets with a heavy stone tied to his neck to pull down his head and show the hair shaved in the shape of the hated cross.

A Catholic seen wearing a crucifix was arrested by the Guards and tied to a cross to be tormented with hot irons.

As Bibles were searched out of homes and burned in huge bonfires, a new slogan gained popularity. It was "the three haves and the three have-nots," meaning the people should have Mao's picture, Mao's thoughts, and Mao's Little Red Book and abandon God, incense burning, and the offering of paper taels.

Bulldozing Religions

By this time, the visionary Red Guards began to compete with each other. The scramble for power resulted in the formation of many rival groups such as Spring Thunder, Ground Command, Doctrine Guards, Red Banner, Revolutionary Rebels, Red Iron Fighters, Grand Rebel Army, Alliance Command, East Wind, and Proletariat Revolutionaries. The competition between the groups resulted in more savage attacks on anything that stood in their way.

Wanting to outdo each other, they began frantically destroying family shrines, idols, and temples. The China Buddhist Association, the Taoism headquarters on Tiger-Dragon Mountain in Canton, and all sorts of superstitious practices became their target for fame and glory. Moreover, Confucius was denounced as a "devil and a snake."

The violent purges resulted in the official liquidation of open church activities. The Guards even closed down all the regular administrative machinery of the Three-Self Movement and the Patriotic Association of Chinese Catholics. The Religious Affairs Bureau fell along with the rest.

Looking Over the Wall

The fanatical Red Guards soon spread their "fame" outside China. Jurgen Dennert, who spent one month touring China at the height of the Red Guard activity, gives the following eye-witness account as it appeared in *Life* magazine:

Through the streets rolled trucks jam-packed with students dressed in yellow, shabby khaki uniforms or in blue or gray pants with white shirts. Their hair was cut short and they sang revolutionary songs. In each truck one boy beat a large red drum with full force while others operated huge brass instruments and a Chinese tom-tom that produces high, whining tones.

The shrieking of the brass and the beating of the drums seemed to take the breath out of the city. At important road crossings there were loudspeaker cars spewing revolutionary slogans like bullets at the thick crowds. "Down with . . . down with . . . down with. . . ." Every few blocks an agitator exhorted the people. Street signs must be pasted over, the old names changed. The "Street of Golden Calmness" is renamed the "Street of Anti-Imperialism;" the "Street of Poetry" becomes the "Street of Support for the Freedom Fight of the Vietnamese People."

Down the street came a procession of fifty children between eight and ten years old. They carried short sticks, pieces of iron, willow twigs, or leather straps. In the middle of the procession an old woman staggered. The children beat her and kicked her with their feet when she fell. The procession passed by a road crossing where three policemen were on duty. Would they intervene? I wondered. Unperturbed, they stopped the traffic in order to let the procession pass.

. . . Across the alley from where Lo and I were dining one night was a workshop. Through its window we could see about fifty people, some of them members of the Red Guard. Three old men were brought in. They were put into white robes on which large black characters were written.

Lo translated: "We are capitalists and have robbed the people." Red Guard girls put three-foot-high pointed white paper hats on the heads of the old men, who were then forced to kneel and confess their "crimes against the people."

. . . In Wuhan, an industrial city of 2.5 million people on the Yangtze in Central China, the Red Guards were also on the march. Like angels of death, they hurried through the streets and silently entered a building. The victims awaited them apathetically. A gesture—they kneel down. The terrible hat is put on their heads and broad banners describing their deeds are placed on their chests and backs. . . . Once I saw—I could almost touch him—a Christian priest surrounded by Guards. They had put a white robe over his clerical vestments and tied a piece of wood around his neck so that his head was forced down at an angle of almost 90°. The top of the dunce cap pointed ahead like an arrow. Behind him were a group of ten to twelve people, probably part of his parish. I could see their faces very clearly—an expression of despondency, visible even beneath the black lacquer which the Communists had smeared on their faces.[18]

Two young Australians who lived to tell the story described what the Red Guard attack upon religion involved:

. . . in August . . . in the major cities, the clergy were ordered to return to their native villages, the religious buildings were shorn of any architectural and ornamental features which the Red Guards found objectionable, antireligious propaganda was put up on the walls, and every church, mosque, temple and monastery was "secularized." In Shanghai, Siccawei, the famous Catholic cathedral, lost its proud Gothic spires and became a fruit warehouse; at least one mosque was converted into offices, the international church and the Protestant cathedral were occupied by Red Guard groups.

Another poster was addressed to all "Catholics, Protestants, Buddhists and Moslems" and started off "You rolling eggs, religious people . . ." going on to accuse them of deceiving the people, sheltering spies and opposing Chairman Mao's thought. Outside a Catholic church I found an exhibition of anti-Christian propaganda showing missionaries as vilest of hypocrites. In one of the few instances I encountered of direct rudeness I was told by a surly youth to move on, as the pictures on the wall were "China's internal affair."

A front-page article in Hong Kong's leading English newspaper declared: "Christianity in Shanghai comes to an end." The Shanghai correspondent continued to report:

> The final page of the history of Christian religion in Shanghai was written on August 24.
> On that day all the churches, active and inactive, whether conducted by their meager congregations or preserved by the Shanghai Municipal Bureau of Religious Cults, were stripped of the crosses, statues, icons, decorations, and all church paraphernalia by the revolutionary students, wearing Red Guard armbands and determined to eradicate all traces of imperialist, colonial and feudal regimes.

Christmas bells were deathly silent in December. There were no celebration services. All the churches were closed, Bibles burned, ministers and Christian leaders attacked, humiliated, dispersed, punished, and silenced. Under the fury of the young hoodlums, there was no room in the "inn" for the Lord of love.
A Christian student in central China wrote:

> This is a very dangerous time for us. We can only walk the way of the cross. Don't be agitated. Pray for us. . . . We don't know the future. We only know that God rules.[19]

Checkmate!

Those who were bewildered that God would allow a Communist takeover in the first place must have been really confused by now. It was bad enough that the atheistic regime gained organizational control of all the religions (as we saw in the previous chapter). But why did God allow this wholesale raging liquidation and persecution?

Satan may have thought that since he won the battle, he also won the war. He couldn't have been more wrong! God was in control all the time.

For more than 4,000 years China steeped herself in idolatry and superstitions (remember the theistic population explosion we discussed in chapter 2?). For this basic reason, Christianity kept running into dead ends.

The Bible clearly teaches that God hates idolatry. The Israelites were repeatedly told to wage war on idolatrous nations. In China's case, our Lord allowed the Red Guards to root out, to pull down, to destroy, and to throw down so He could build and plant.

Therefore, one of the two main accomplishments of the Cultural Revolution in God's plan is the leveling off of all religions. Christianity now has an even footing and will get an even start in the new race for the Chinese heart. Even the present "down with Confucianism" movement is actually very much in accord with this theme. Praise God!

This is fine so far, but what about the true Church? They were involved in the bloodbath, too. How is that justified?

To begin with, we must realize that while suffering often bears a negative connotation, it has many positive aspects. Again and again it is seen in the Word of God as a blessing in disguise.

It is not my intention to sound pious nor my desire to just be optimistic. I believe suffering, pain, agony, and even death can often be "disguised blessings," because the Lord has allowed me to personally experience the true meaning of Romans 8:28.

A little over a year ago, when I was preaching in New Zealand, I received a phone call which told me my little daughter was rushed into the hospital because of a bicycle accident. The man on the other end of the line said, "Silas, she has been severely injured and the condition is not good."

I could not believe what I heard at first. Then I simply refused to accept the facts. So I went to my room, closed the door, and immediately prayed. I asked the Lord to heal my child and give her back to me. I said, "Lord, how could this possibly be happening? Even if it is serious, I know You can perform miracles. After all, I did pray for their safety and Your protection on the family before I left the house. I prayed for them when I was in the taxi, when I was on the plane, and since I got here. I have asked You daily to watch over them. How could this possibly happen!"

My prayers and my thoughts proved one thing—that is, I considered the whole event a gruesome, tragic misfortune from which no good could come.

Upon returning home the next day, as I stood by my daughter's bedside in the hospital I discovered, first of all, God did protect her. You see, although she was hit by a car while riding her bike, there was not a broken bone, not a single drop of blood shed, and not even a slight scratch on her entire body. God simply touched her brain and took her home; and since the brain cannot feel pain, Tanya left this world without feeling a bit of discomfort. I asked the Lord to protect her from pain, from danger, and from death; but the Lord protected her in harm, in pain, in danger, and even in death.

As I calmed down considerably, my wife reminded me of the prayers Tanya used to say. I then recalled how she often included this in her evening prayer: "Dear heavenly Father, I want to see You when I'm young, not when I'm all grown up."

In these occasions as I tucked them in to sleep, little Tanya repeated the same prayer many times. We tried to explain to her that Jesus would be coming soon and we would all be seeing him together—sort of a "family plan." But she insisted on repeating the same thing. Sometimes she would look up at me and try to explain what she meant: "Daddy, do you know why I want to see Jesus while I'm young? Because when I'm all grown up I won't be able to fit on His lap anymore."

As I now look back, I begin to understand why the Lord impressed that thought upon her. It is God's plan that we should be comforted by these words even today.

As we went through her things later, we discovered there were seven dollars left behind. Since Tanya was a tither, I thought it was quite significant. So I commented to my wife, "Well, that's pretty good—seven dollars for seven years." But then I realized she was more than seven years old. When my wife told me she was seven years and five months, I immediately felt there should be five coins in her little purse. I ran upstairs and opened up her wallet, and sure enough, there were five coins in it.

This fingerprint of God (and many others) proved to me without a shadow of a doubt that God had a plan for little Tanya. Seven dollars and five coins for seven years and five months. May I say, if God had a plan for a little life like Tanya's, he certainly has great plans for China and her millions.

The disguised blessings were not realized when I conducted the graveside service. They became obvious weeks later. Because of Tanya's home-going, the next-door Catholic lady came to ask my wife the way of salvation. Because of this, Sonya led her cousin and two neighborhood friends to the Lord. Today there is a Bible study being held at our home for parents in the neighborhood and of the nearby school. Furthermore, the Tanya Hong Memorial Scholarship Fund is benefiting children who cannot afford elementary Christian education.

Since the so-called tragedy we have all been ushered into a deeper relationship with the Lord, and in this way we are drawn closer to Tanya as well. And we are looking forward more earnestly than ever to the coming of our Redeemer.

Sure enough, there were a lot of tears and sleepless nights. Even to this very day I often wake up in the morning and cannot go back to sleep because the things Tanya did keep coming to mind. But all in all, we can sincerely praise and thank the Lord for all that He has done.

Truly the Chinese church has suffered beyond description under Communism, but I can clearly see how all things are working together for God in China to those who love the Lord.

The Bible assures us in 1 Peter 4:

12. Beloved, think it not strange concerning the fiery trial which is to try you, as though some strange thing happened unto you:

13. But rejoice, inasmuch as ye are partakers of Christ's sufferings; that, when his glory shall be revealed, ye may be glad also with exceeding joy.

14. If ye be reproached for the name of Christ, happy are ye; for the spirit of glory and of God resteth upon you: on their part he is evil spoken of, but on your part he is glorified.

17. For the time is come that judgment must begin at the house of God: and if it first begin at us, what shall the end be of them that obey not the gospel of God?

If you want another reference, here it is. Matthew 5:10–12:

10. Blessed are they which are persecuted for righteousness' sake: for their's is the kingdom of heaven.

11. Blessed are ye, when men shall revile you, and persecute you, and shall say all manner of evil against you falsely, for my sake.

12. Rejoice, and be exceeding glad: for great is your reward in heaven: for so persecuted they the prophets which were before you.

The purifying fire of Communism has burned away the "rice Christians" and refined the believers into golden vessels of honor. You can be sure that they will be the ones playing the major role in future evangelism in China.

The late Chiang Kai shek said: "In China today, there are countless instances of unpublicized Christian martyrdom at the hands of communism. From the blood of such martyrdom will spring the seeds of the reborn China which will arise in the future."[20]

The Bible is absolutely correct when it states in Romans 8:28 that all things work together for good to them that love God, to them who are the called according to His purpose.

Just before our Lord Jesus Christ endured the cross upon which He suffered more than anyone, He referred to the spiritual battle with the enemy and the certain victory by saying:

> . . . upon this rock I will build my church; and the gates of hell shall not prevail against it (Matthew 16:18).

5

Language Reform and Evangelism

Go to, let us go down, and there confound their language,
that they may not understand one another's speech.

Genesis 11:7

The Communist regime has had a tremendous impact on another vital part of Chinese life—the language. The story of how they once again unascertainably paved the way for evangelism is the thrilling subject of this chapter.

If you chanced to open and examine one of China's current propaganda magazines like *China Reconstructs, People's Pictorial,* or the *Peking Review,* you would undoubtedly discover these characters:

1. 从 (follow) 2. 胜 (overcome) 3. 卩 (protect)
4. 儿 (son) 5. 进 (enter)

Now compare the above simplified new script with these identical words in their old form:

1. 從 (follow) 2. 勝 (overcome) 3. 衛 (protect)
4. 兒 (son) 5. 進 (enter)

You can easily see radical changes have been made in the Chinese written language. Although not every simplified character is as drastically different from the old as these, most of them have undergone considerable alteration since the takeover. According to reliable sources, the Party has simplified approximately one-fourth of all the Chinese characters so far.

In the examples above, the word *follow* has been reduced from eleven strokes to four. The word *protect* simplified from fifteen to three. Since Chinese words (characters) are all constructed with various strokes, one would have to admit that it is much easier to learn the new.

Tongues Tied

Recently in New York City, I interviewed a twenty-six-year-old fellow who had just escaped from China. In the course of our conversation, which was in one of China's major dialects—Cantonese, I questioned him about language reform. My main interest was to confirm that Mao's program had achieved a degree of success as other refugees and China visitors told me.

The young man said Mandarin (the official national language) was not only promoted in the schools in Canton, it was the only acceptable tongue in certain classes. He further assured me that the common dialect *(p'u-t'ung hua),* which is Mandarin with a native accent, can be understood by the average Cantonese without any difficulty.

I couldn't help remembering my own experience in Canton twenty-seven years ago. When we first moved to the city, my parents' northern language was grossly inadequate in the market places. I can still remember how they had to point and gesture to get the plumpest duck hanging in the window at the most reasonable price.

Inspired by the humorous adage, "Don't be afraid of heaven or earth, but do fear a Cantonese speaking the official dialect," I began talking Mandarin to him to see what would happen. To my surprise, he switched just as quickly and came out with beautiful Mandarin.

On another occasion a twenty-three-year-old escapee, who had slipped out under the Bamboo Curtain just months before coming to Los Angeles, told me he was able to use Mandarin while traveling from Canton in the south all the way to Heilungkiang in the north during the Cultural Revolution. He, too, spoke very good Mandarin.

Judging from testimonials like these, it is apparent that Mao's dialect reform has been very successful, at least among the young. Mao has truly tamed the Chinese tongues!

A Picture's Worth a Thousand Words

To be sure, such accomplishment was not easily achieved. Thousands of years ago etymologists, lexicographers, and the like began weaving the tangled web by devising a complicated pictorial written system.

In the beginning, when the Chinese wanted to record things like *sun, moon, mountain, stream,* and *person,* they did it like this:

⊙   ☽   Ⅿ   ⫯⫯   ⏽

These minipictures eventually evolved to this present form:

日   月   山   川   人

Soon they began combining these simple pictures for greater expression. They put *sun* 日 and *moon* 月 together to make the new word: 明 *bright.* They used two trees 林 to represent *forest* or *grove,* and three trees 森 for *luxuriant vegetation.*

While we are on the subject of putting words together, here are a couple I know you will find very interesting. When the Chinese made the word *good,* a girl 女 and a boy 子 are joined like so: 好 . Doesn't this remind you of Genesis 2:18? There God said, "It is not good that the man should be alone."

Here's another one: 臭 . We have two characters, one on top of the other. They are *self* 自 and *big* 大 . The interesting thing about this word is the little dot on the upper right of *big* 大 . You see 臭 means *stink.* Can you guess what the hidden lesson is? They are trying to say that one iota of "self bigness" smells; too much of "self" stinks. Isn't this what the Bible teaches?

Naturally, the limited pictures and their combinations were still inadequate and the need for other methods of creating words was obvious. So they began building stories into the characters. Two examples of this, *ship* 船 and *come* 來 have already been examined in the first chapter.

Then, the pictorial basis began to expand into abstract and symbolic fashion. You will have to employ a bit of imagination to appreciate the following two examples of ideography:

刃　　Here an additional stroke is added to the knife to accent its sharpness. The word means *blade.*

本　　A small horizontal stroke is placed near the bottom of the tree. What does it mean? It shows the roots and translates as *origin* or *source.*

In order to further illustrate the complexity of the characters, I want to introduce you to another category. It is the radicals and specifiers. At this stage they began borrowing classifiers to make new words. For instance, 疒 specifies *illness* or *disease*. When you put 丙 with it, you make 病 which means *sickness.* If you put 豆 instead, you will get *smallpox* 痘. That little character 豆 by itself means *beans,* to illustrate the accompanying rash.

In this manner one part of the character serves as the sounding element while the other part indicates the basic meaning of the word. The following are good samples:

坊 (a ward) 訪 (to visit) 紡 (to spin) 肪 (animal fat). Unfortunately, the position of the radicals varies. It could be on the bottom of the word or off to the left. To make a complicated matter more perplexing, the specifiers do not always indicate the basic meaning.

As years went by compound words multiplied. In addition, some characters appeared with an amazing number of strokes, such as 灑 (to sprinkle water) with twenty-five and 灘 (the manner of flowing water) with twenty-seven.

The complexity of the script which resulted in the high illiteracy rate produced a deep sense of respect for the printed pages. In the old days there were laws which prohibited trademarks on the bottom of the shoes.

As a little boy, I used to hear my grandmother tell me that a golden house and a beautiful wife can both be found in the books. She said, "Fame, prestige, enjoyment, and wealth are hidden between the covers of the books." And she herself was illiterate.

Well, so much for the Chinese words. Aren't you glad you don't have to learn them?

Watch Your Language

By now you are expert enough to know that written Chinese is not a phonetic system which spells out the sounds. This makes it necessary for the student to memorize each stroke in every word. Furthermore, he must imitate each sound and retain it by heart. That's why so many Chinese couldn't read or write;

and those who could write often made mistakes in their calligraphy.

Pronunciation is made even more difficult because of the phonetic poverty of the language. It has fewer than 500 different syllables with which to communicate. This created the problem of overcrowding meanings into sounds. For instance, the sound *ma* can mean four different things in Mandarin and six in Cantonese, depending on the tone it is given. This is why many Caucasians feel one has to be musically inclined to speak Chinese.

Due to geographical diversity, the five main tongues (Mandarin, Wu, Min, Hakka, and Cantonese) comprise hundreds of variations which have developed into dialects with independent systems of pronunciation.

Let's take the simple word 三 *three*. The people in Peking pronounce it *szan*, the folks in Canton say *saam*, those living in Shanghai express it as *saih* while the Szechwanese change it to *san*.

Although it would be unfair to convey the idea that there are no similarities in the dialects, it is still accurate to emphasize the tremendous difficulty in trying to communicate across dialectical boundaries. Interpreters were used all the time to get the speaker's message through.

Tower of Babel Revisited

China was hopelessly fragmented by the hundreds of different tongues spoken within her confines. She was analogized as a plate of scattered sand—disunited and individualistic. For this reason, this four-thousand-year-old nation has only recently joined the nuclear club. After all, if you cannot understand each other, how could you work together as a team? And without a team, how can you join the league?

To prove how effectively language can divide people, read these verses from Genesis 11:

And the Lord came down to see the city and the tower, which the children of men builded.

And the Lord said, Behold, the people is one, and they have all one language; and this they begin to do: and now nothing will be restrained from them, which they have imagined to do.

Go to, let us go down, and there confound their language, that they may not understand one another's speech.

So the Lord scattered them abroad from thence upon the face of all the earth: and they left off to build the city.

Genesis 11:5–8

A Problem of Antiquity

The Middle Kingdom has known for hundreds of years that she had a language problem. This is demonstrated in the first authorized reform way back in the Ch'in dynasty (third century B.C.) when a "small seal" style appeared. Specifiers were somewhat brought under control and some characters received their simplified forms. For example, 藂 was changed to 集 .

During the Han dynasty about the time the Christian era was beginning, more simplified words surfaced and "cursive script" grew.

Then in the Ming dynasty (fourteenth century) efforts were again revived to grapple with the problem. But no sooner had they gotten under way when the opposition began operating. Teachers were against simplifying the characters and prohibited their students from using easier forms. They even went so far as to fail them in their exams for abbreviating the script. Needless to say, conservatism prevailed.

Later attempts to introduce the theory of romanization via missionaries were also thwarted. These Western efforts made very little difference in the Chinese language.

When the first republic was established on the mainland in 1912, there was renewed enthusiasm for producing a simpler script and nationalized language. Unfortunately, because of wars and internal unrest the project never reached a full scale.

However, in the year 1915, a significant language reform movement took place. A man by the name of Hu Shih spearheaded the "plain language" or *bái húa* movement. He promoted the so-called eight-not campaign in his draft of literature reform. In spite of strong opposition, the idea of abolishing classic literary style *(wen yan)* in favor of plain language gained popularity and eventual acceptance.

Communist Characters

Ever since the Communists began their revolution in the early 20s, they, too, purposed to do something about the language problems. Their original idea was not to simplify the characters as we saw at the beginning of the chapter. They actually wanted to abolish them completely. It was their intent to romanize the entire written language by using an alphabetical system.

After the establishment of the People's Republic of China in 1949, and subsequent to five years of intensive study, planning, and debating, the first National Conference on Language Reform was held in October of 1955. The Ministry of Education and the Committee on Language Reform summoned 207 representatives from all over China representing all walks of life to discuss the complex problem.

The conference was followed by hundreds of committees and meetings to discuss reform in-depth.

Finally the Scientific Conference on the Problems of Standardizing Modern Spoken Chinese concluded that an alphabetical script with sound values for its symbols was impossible without a unified national spoken language. In other words, the hundreds of dialects had to go before an alphabetical system could be devised. That's a pretty big order, isn't it?

So a three-year survey of the country's hundreds of tongues was conducted to promote the common dialect *(P'u t'ung hua)*. This impressive endeavor covered 1,188 geographical locations in twenty-three provinces.

The difficulties in combining all the dialects and establishing a nationalized language required some of the best men in the business to tackle the problem. They included professional writers, translators, actors, broadcasters, newsmen, and publishers.

Although there was still a minority arguing for immediate

adoption of an alphabetical system and abolishment of the characters, the consensus of opinion went against them. Most people felt it would be criminal to destroy China's rich cultural heritage embodied in the characters.

The head of the National Academy of Science, Kuo Mo-jo, defended the case well by saying:

> For 4,000 years the characters have made very great contributions to Chinese culture and to the cultural life of the Chinese people. An absolutely major part of our extremely rich and treasurable cultural heritage has been preserved by records in the characters. Even today and for a long time to come, in our task of building socialism, we still have to depend on the characters as media for culture and education as a means of communication in social life. The fact that the characters possess a brilliant, glorious history has been witnessed by all.[21]

Along the same line, the Chairman of the National Committee on Language Reform, Wu Yu-chang explained that the characters would be used by the immense population as a means for reading and writing.

The final curtain was drawn when Premier Chou voiced the official policy: "While we search for a phonetic system for the Chinese language in the distant future, efforts will be directed to the simplification of the written characters."

Consequently, early in 1956 the State Council in Peking ratified lists of 515 drastically simplified characters. The historic transition had officially started!

Later Chou went a step further by explaining that phonetic spelling *(pīnyīn)* would play a subservient role:

> Our promotion of the p'u-t'ung hua (common language) aims at the removal of the barriers among the dialects but not at the suppression or destruction of the dialects.
>
> I must first of all make clear that the phonetic system will be one that serves as a system of notations to the pronunciation of the characters; it will also help promote the general

adoption of a common spoken language. But it will definitely not be used as a phonetic script to replace the characters. The primary purpose of the phonetic system is to serve as notations to the pronunciation of the characters.[22]

This explains why out of the 50 million people who were reported to have become literate in 1958, only 10 percent had learned phonetic spelling.

Expediting Evangelism

In 1942, Mao taught that literature must form a part of the revolutionary machinery. Why was he so interested in the promotion of literacy? So more and more people could read and digest his Communist propaganda. He hoped this would mold China into a united socialistic state.

Why was he so enthusiastic about cultivating a common dialect? Because if language can divide, it can also unite.

Can God's program benefit by what Mao and the boys have done? Read on and judge for yourself!

Throughout history the Lord has used the written word to convey His message of love and redemption. In Exodus 32:15, 16, we learn the two tablets given Moses on Mount Sinai were inscribed with ". . . the writing of God." When the king of Babylon feasted with the vessels from the temple in Jerusalem, God delivered His message with the handwriting on the wall. When Jesus was asked to judge the adulterous woman, He stooped down and wrote on the ground. In Revelation 1:11 John is commanded, "What thou seest, write in a book, and send it unto the seven churches. . . ."

The importance of the written word in evangelism cannot be overexaggerated. Because the Bible is the inspired Word of God given to men, Robert Morrison spent more than twelve years in translation so a Chinese could read it for himself. And since then, the New Testament has been retranslated or revised an average of every eight years! The Old Testament every ten!

Prior to 1949, the Bible was a closed book to multiplied millions of illiterate Chinese; but today if the Word of God is placed in the hands of the average person on the mainland, he can read it! What a tremendous challenge! Communism's promotion of literacy has paved the way for a literature crusade for Christ on an unprecedented scale in the Middle Kingdom!

Now, what about the unified dialect? How does it expedite evangelism?

In the past when "the Chinese Billy Graham," Dr. John Sung, spoke in evangelistic meetings, he would regularly have to speak through an interpreter. Sometimes he even preached in English. Doesn't that sound strange? A Chinese (whose native tongue was Chinese) speaking to his own people in his own country using an interpreter to translate his English?

You've heard the expression, "It loses a lot in translation." Well, not much will be getting lost any more. The body of Jesus Christ in China can now witness to a greater number of people wherever they are sent. The language barriers have been broken down.

Not only that, Mandarin was chosen as the common language because it is softer, less gutteral, and not hard to hear or repeat. This "official dialect" has less tones to each sound. The 400 basic monosyllables multiplied by their four tones gives us a maximum of only 1,600 separate items. So of course it would be less difficult for a foreigner to learn.

If, Lord willing, the Bamboo Curtain should lift to allow foreign missionaries to return, they would have a much easier time with the spoken word! Especially when the new standard Roman spellings are adopted (it seems they are going to be) by the government.

Crossroads

Mao has given China's millions his Little Red Book and preached that Communism is the answer. God has given us His Word where it says Christ is ". . . the Way, the Truth, the Life. . . ."

What book will they be reading? To whom will they be listening?

Will the 800 million people be fed only the diet of atheism?

Certainly the One who doesn't wish even one single soul to perish has definitely allowed the simplification and unification of China's language for a good purpose—evangelism at large in the near future.

6
Psyched Out. . . .

There is a way that seemeth right unto a man, but the end thereof are the ways of death.

Proverbs 16:25

By the time of the takeover, the membership of the Communist Party in China had grown from 40 thousand to 1.5 million. Isn't that a pretty impressive figure? What do you suppose is the reason they grew so rapidly?

The answer to the question is a complicated one because many factors need to be taken into consideration. However, one fundamental reason was their effective propaganda program aimed at the lower-middle class. Mao got off on the right foot by training his secret agents to tell the people exactly what they wanted to hear.

Through these mouthpieces, Mao gained support by sympathizing with his countrymen and promising that things would be a lot better if they followed his leadership. He pledged to play the role of Robin Hood by robbing from the rich and giving to the poor. He vowed to equally divide the landlords' houses, fields, money, and goods among the people.

Pretty attractive bait, isn't it?

To make it even more tempting, he added these lures to the line: the promise of more food, better working conditions, and a share-and-share-alike policy.

On October 1, 1949, he reeled in his prize trophy and labeled it The People's Republic of China. What was he trying to prove? By adding People's to the old title Republic of China, by naming the currency the "people's" money, and by calling the military the People's Liberation Army, he was proclaiming that China belonged to the proletariat. It is easy to guess that many hearts were warmed by his masterful psychological play.

Mao further strummed the heartstrings of the masses by pronouncing these famous words: "We have stood up!" Among the cheering and applauding crowds many no doubt echoed the words in their minds. It felt good to know that China belonged to the masses. It was quite a shot in the arm!

Their glee was understandable when you consider that for centuries China was exploited by outsiders. I still remember how Shanghai was divided according to the countries who "borrowed" her land. Before the independence of Mongolia, China's shape exactly resembled a mulberry leaf. And it is a fitting analogy that foreign "silkworms" had been feeding on it for much too long. The Chinese pride would welcome a change.

The people were optimistic about the new government. Perhaps Communism was the answer to all their problems. The polite behavior of the troops, their parsimonious living style, and meticulous efficiency were all quite impressive.

Hundred Flowers Movement

As time went by, in the eyes of the victorious leader things were really looking great. He had spent four years shaping up the country by ousting missionaries and other foreigners and eliminating "bad guys" through agrarian reform and other bloody campaigns.

By the time the first five-year plan (1953–1957) was about over and the streets and homes were cleaned up, Mao felt safe enough to do a little mind-cleaning. Borrowing a phrase from the Chinese classics, he said, "Let a hundred flowers bloom and let a hundred schools of thought contend."

This Hundred Flowers Movement, which began in mid-1956, was the most liberal campaign ever launched by the regime. Mao was hoping to harness the voices of the intellectuals in favor of Marxism-Leninism. Since high-school graduates were lumped into this category, it affected a considerable number of people.

The attempt to sweep away obstacles in Communism's way with words got off to a very slow start because people were reluctant to speak their minds freely. In order to encourage participation, Mao delivered his most famous post-1949 speech on February 27, 1957 called, "On the Correct Handling of Contradictions Among the People."

Finally, by May, things really started hopping. Some harsh and frank criticism quickly erupted. Wall posters denouncing every aspect of the government appeared. The intelligensia, Three-Self Movement leaders, and the public in general all got into the act. Rather than emphasizing particular defects within the system, the critics challenged the leadership and the Chinese Communist Party itself.

The scientists responded by recommending the Scientific Planning Commission be abolished and the Academy of Sciences be restored to primacy. They wanted to separate politics from science and complained that they had excessive political and administrative duties which hindered study and research.

Teachers and students complained of extensive Party supervision. They felt selection and promotion of students should be based on academic achievement rather than political qualifications.

The public complained about food shortages and lack of personal freedom while religious leaders accused the government's Three-Self Movement of trying to annihilate Christianity.

The Three-Self Movement's vice-chairman, Marcus Cheng, also voiced criticism of the government. He denounced various arms of the dictatorship for interfering in the lives of Christians. He also maintained it was wrong to prohibit the resumption of services in small cities and villages and keep the confiscated buildings and furniture. His main gripe was that policy was not uniform and some cadres were hostile toward church donations, buildings, and new members. Then he concluded by criticizing the antireligious literature current in the country.

Bishop Ting, Communist sympathizer, addressed the Union Theological Seminary in Nanking, attacking atheism itself. He explained that Communism tries to divide all systems of thought into two categories: materialism and idealism. Then they condemn the latter and approve the former. However, Ting pointed out that Christianity is neither—not the fruit of history or an ideology. It is a free revelation of God. This is perhaps the most remarkable and forthright statement made when the flowers of criticism bloomed in China. Why? Because it gives us a quick glimpse at the depth of the true believer's heart who was later forced to bend with the wind.

Picking the Blossoms

Before the flowers had a chance to fully bloom, pruning scissors were ready for them. The campaign was abruptly ended before May was over because things had gotten out of hand. Without wasting any time, the regime immediately transformed the Hundred Flowers Movement into an antirightest campaign. Critics were subjected to severe denunciation through brainwashing, indoctrination, imprisonment, demotion, and similar techniques.

For the first time, the general populace openly felt the treachery of atheistic tactics. It was apparent that the so-called freedom in the People's Republic was either a bait or a mockery.

To this day, the lesson has not been forgotten. Foreign visitors still find it difficult to communicate meaningfully with the mainland Chinese. Most people won't open up; and those who do would only voice the opinion acceptable to the Party line. Can you blame them? After all, they paid a tremendous price for less than a month of "free" speech.

However, the Party paid, too. The entire leadership was convulsed by this episode. The impact was particularly damaging for Mao who thought it up in the first place. He lost the chairmanship of the Party Secretariat and needed to come up with a new strategy to bolster his image.

Back to the Drawing Board

In order to combat poor harvests and sluggish industrialization, the leaders focused their attention on China's ace in the hole, the tremendous resource of manpower. Under the slogan TWENTY YEARS IN A DAY, they would try to achieve pure Communism in one tremendous leap—the Great Leap Forward.

The first step was to establish industrial communes in the larger cities to increase industrial output. Thousands of students and teachers were sent to the factories to help in the construction of blast furnaces. Out in the countryside, farmers were getting into the act. A system of producing pig iron in their backyard furnaces was instituted to try to alleviate the tremendous shortage of iron.

In addition, thousands of students were "volunteered" for road building, reservoir constructing, and dike erecting.

Next, Peking's Central Committee issued a special directive ordering an elaborate system of agricultural communes. Private lots were taken and ownership of acreage was transferred to much larger units. Astoundingly, 95 percent of the peasantry were involved in four short months. All in all, 50 thousand communes were set up during this period which might well be called the world's most drastic agricultural reform ever.

The tremendous maneuver of relocating and reshuffling people drastically altered the normal life-style. Nevertheless, enthusiasm mounted at first. It seemed for a brief period that Mao had found the secret of implementing successful Communism in pulling the country up by her own bootstraps.

Communal Living

As the fires in the backyard furnaces burned, it singed the four-thousand-year-old tradition of close family life. Husbands and wives were separated and their children left in communal nursery facilities while mothers pursued more "productive" jobs. Home-cooked meals became a thing of the past as people crammed into dining halls for their food.

In most cases, communal food was given as part of the wage system. Others were so eager to reach the final stage of "giving according to abilities," they began offering free haircuts, free clothing, and so forth. Privately owned pots, pans, and knives were confiscated to use as scrap iron; and even nails in the walls were pulled out and used for the cause.

Ashes from the Fire

Because of the rapid change in life-style, horrible weaknesses showed up in the communal system. The program had gone through the real test and proved miserably wanting. Mao was forced by public sentiment to approve modifications to his own brainchild.

Because consumption under the "free" system in the communes had soared, the giveaway had to stop. Personal communized items were ordered returned to their owners. Private plots were again permitted in some areas and farmers were allowed to grow their own food and keep poultry and pigs for themselves. Apart from exceptional cases, people returned to their homes for dinner, but ten homes had to share one kitchen knife.

In addition, private enterprise was allowed in professions ranging from doctors to barbers. Even black market prices were legalized and called "free markets" for the "richer" to buy rice and other staples.

Suddenly there was a capitalistic ray of hope. Dirty rickshaws were cleaned and fixed up by their owners. Hillsides which had been left untilled were being plowed. Although some communes still persisted in a few areas, the "magnificent madness" was slowly regaining its sanity.

What did it all prove?

First of all, the backyard furnaces proved a waste of time. The iron they produced was totally unfit for industrial use. The economy became so badly crippled that production dropped by more than 40 percent between 1959 to 1962.

Second, the communal fiasco created great agricultural disasters. Officers in charge lied on their reports of accomplishments to avoid criticism, demotion, and possible imprisonment. But the actual situation was clearly stated when Chou En-lai told Edgar Snow that the grain production in 1960 had fallen far below the new targets. He said it was in fact worse than the previous two years.

Severe food shortages and the threat of famine caused relatives in Hong Kong to send twelve million food packages in to fend off starvation.

Third, things began to deteriorate rapidly between China and her big brother, the USSR. When the Soviets and Eastern European nations began ridiculing the communal failures, the ideological rift widened. Soviet technicians and advisors were finally withdrawn. The absence of Soviet economic assistance and technical advice made matters worse.

Fourth, it proved that the strong family ties were more binding than any Communist coercion. China was not ready to sacrifice the family system for the "people." After all, it has been the fundamental unit which has withstood the test of time.

Mao must have been really sweating in his "boiler suit" when he finished his great leap. (No wonder he took the famous swim!)

To heap coals on the fire, 60 thousand Chinese streamed across the border into Hong Kong within a few weeks' time in 1962. This famous May exodus was another slap in the face for the leader who had lost his presidency of the People's Republic during this period of the second five-year plan.

Mao Fever

If there was any way Mao could top the colossal mistakes of the past, it was definitely the Cultural Revolution. We have already seen in the fourth chapter how he instigated and promoted full-scale national anarchy. Under the guise of putting the "four olds" to the torch, Mao wanted to silence his critics and purge the ranks of those less radical than he.

By the height of his revolution, his dream was coming true. Millions of teenagers, wearing Mao pins and arm bands inscribed with the words *Hung wei bing* (Red Guard) in the leader's own handwriting, were running rampant all over the country.

As Mao once again basked in the sunlight of popularity, his Little Red Book became the "bible" of China. It was found in every home. In the countryside, it was the first book some households ever had. It was the bread and water for the young; and everyone was ordered to read it or have it read aloud. The book became the cohesive force that temporarily welded China together.

Intensive study of Mao's works by the whole Party and nation was of important historical significance. Mao was exalted as the greatest Marxist-Leninist of our era and a genius in inheriting, defending, and developing Marxism-Leninism.

While the mercury in the thermometer rose, so did the passion of the Red Guards. The nine tumultuous rallies of the power-drunk youth astounded even Peking. Fourteen million of the young vigilantes paraded outside the Tien An gate. Perhaps it was the glowing radiance of the sun which inspired them to refer to Mao as the Red Sun in their hearts.

This little song became so popular that I even learned it while living in Hong Kong:

> From the red east rises the sun
> In China appears Mao Tse-tung.
> He works for the people's welfare,
> He is the people's great savior.

> The Communist Party is like the sun,
> Wherever it shines there is light;
> Where the Communist Party goes,
> There the people are liberated.

In Shao-shan, Mao's birthplace, he appeared in a portrait as the savior, wearing a white robe and sandals with a rosy glow radiating from him.

A Chinese poet expressed his worship like this:

> When the Chairman walks across the land,
> The hills and many waters dance;
> The Yellow River, tail wagging, chants;
> And Mount Omei proffers tribute with open hand.

> When the Chairman walks across the land,
> Workers and peasants joyfully arise;
> Hills of grain and cotton split the skies;
> Iron and steel in a mighty stream expand![23]

From Atheism to Maotheism

When Lin Piao wrote the foreword for Mao's Little Red Book,
he probably never dreamed this statement was "prophetic":

> Once Mao Tse-tung's thought is grasped by the broad
> masses, it becomes an inexhaustible source of strength and
> a spiritual atom bomb of infinite power.

The spiritual atom bomb finally exploded into a new ethic
and pseudoreligion. Mao's little red "generals" became the legion of executioners. They believed that "heaven is the Red
Guard's heaven and earth is the Red Guard's earth." As they
persecuted presidents, principals, mayors, teachers, Christians,
or anyone standing in Mao's way, they used to say, "The country
wants me to beat you, and Chairman Mao wants me to beat
you."

The zealous youth had pulled out all the stops and were not
afraid to get their hands dirty. The following statement illustrates their devotion quite graphically:

> We are truly Mao Tse-tung's old yellow cow. We deeply
> till the ground and turn up the fertile soil to allow the seeds
> of Mao Tse-tung to be planted deeply into the field of peo-
> ple's hearts.[24]

But they didn't stop there. Their lives, they felt, were a small
price to pay for their "religion." You don't have to take my
word for it—read this little slogan that says it all:

> If you cut off my head, it's not important
> As long as my ideology is true.
> While I live, I'll closely follow Chairman Mao.
> After I die I'm going to see Marx.[25]

They used to shout, "We don't need any brains! Our heads are
armed with the ideas of Mao Tse-tung." Not only that, at the
peak of Mao worship ardent followers used to "pray" to him

three times a day. They would gather before a giant portrait of their leader in the morning and say words to this effect:

> We thank you, our great leader, for this bright and beautiful day. We thank you for our health with which we can serve our country. Strengthen us now as we march off to work.

At noon before they partook their meal, they would give thanks to Mao for his great leadership which brought them the "delicious" food.

Then, before they retired in the evening, this was their evening prayer:

> Our most respected great leader, we confess that we have failed today because we did not accomplish as much as we wanted to. We realize it is all because we did not study hard enough your teachings and your thoughts.

A Revolting Development

Things really got out of control altogether when the Red Guards began swiping weapons from the army to outdo each other. By January of 1967, the revolutionary rebels had succeeded in seizing power from the Shanghai Party and municipal authorities. Workers who had been enjoying the incentive benefits of "economism" began to fear for their livelihood. So they organized groups to resist the high-handed youths. The civil war caused chaos through massive strikes, industrial sabotage, and paralysis of ports and railroads.

Fighting broke out widely all over the country between the Guards themselves and the workers. China's one hundred million youth swept across thousands of miles and carried on the officially inspired anarchy in mass demonstration. It was certainly without historical parallel.

Mao finally realized that something had to be done to save China from near total destruction. It is reported that Mao literally wept in one instance when he heard of the devastating results of his ingenious "invention." Unfortunately, the few drops of tears were far from sufficient in forming a river of repentance for him to dive in and lead another swim.

Army to the Rescue

By mid-1967 the country's life was approaching a standstill due to the rampant destructive mania. Mao finally had to yield and call on the People's Liberation Army (PLA) to mobilize three million soldiers to control the fanatical Red Guards. He personally ordered all the "little generals" to return to their classrooms and carry on the revolution there. The monster Mao created for his own gain backed him into a corner while his opponents gradually came out of hiding.

The Great Letdown

The young rebels finally realized the initial push had been directed from the highest echelons of the Peking government and was not a spontaneous grass-roots movement after all. Their enthusiasm quickly cooled off with the advent of the army and was replaced by an attitude of indifference and resentment.

After months of being the "law," the troublemakers did not take the back-to-school orders seriously. Instead, they roved around continuing their attacks to destroy as many things as possible. They also indulged themselves in free love, poker playing, and other aspects of dissipated living.

A showdown was inevitable. Conflicts between the Guards and the PLA resulted in another kind of civil war.

The Cultural Revolution tore the fabric of the nation into a three-way faction: the revolutionary masses (Red Guards, hippies and yippies), revolutionary cadres (old loyal Party officials), and the PLA. This stalemate lasted until revolutionary committees were set up throughout the provinces.

Chaotic Classrooms

Since the shutdown of educational institutions, teachers and students found it extremely difficult to resume normal classroom functions.

The kids had tasted the carefree style of living. They developed skill in disrupting and were in no mood to subject themselves to classroom discipline. After all, they had been taught the five "dares"—Dare to think, speak, act, revolt, and riot. And they knew the four "not fears"—Don't fear heaven, earth, God, or ghosts.

Knowing that Mao was only intending to utilize the school premises as detention and relocation centers, many decided to call the army's bluff. On one occasion, twenty students in Canton decided to walk out of the Number 29 Middle School in defiance of the pointed guns. Unfortunately, the soldiers weren't bluffing. They opened fire. A few were killed and others were injured.

Nevertheless, it wasn't until the spring of 1968 that most of the primary students and half of the junior and senior high students were back at their desks.

Teachers, too, were reluctant to resume their posts. They were still smarting from the mistreatment during the national madness. It was hard to forget the humiliation and physical abuse they endured. The memory of their colleagues who were killed or committed suicide was too fresh in their minds. The ones who were ordered to catch crickets for the rebels simply were too embarrassed to stand up and teach.

Those who returned to the classrooms were in no condition to teach or learn. The time was spent having tea parties to welcome new arrivals, discussing nature, and listening to speeches.

As things continued to quiet down, many of the students were sent to rural and remote areas where they couldn't cause trouble. Once there, it was their job to develop the virgin land.

The fate of the whole disastrous crusade and the deification of Mao can be best described by one young leader's expression: *Wanluh*—It is finished.

How Now Red Mao

In the two decades of Mao's leadership, his image gradually deteriorated from the robust revolutionary hero of the famous

Long March to the plump blundering figure who caused the tragic "Nightmare Children's Crusade" as the official Party magazine, *Red Flag,* called it. Not only had he lost popularity, he complained that he was being treated "like a dead parent at a funeral."

The young people were turned off as quickly as they were turned on. While talking to a former Red Guard a couple months ago, he told me how he and his colleagues used to curse the name of Mao while working in the fields. His feelings explain why Mao's portraits were often riddled with bulletholes.

In the years since the Cultural Revolution, the "Red Sun" continues his descent beyond the horizon, never again to warm the hearts of the people. Moreover, his efforts in pushing that boy wonder, Wang Hung-wen, and his militant wife, Chiang Ching, were to no avail.

On November 2, 1974, the Los Angeles *Times* ran a lengthy article titled, "Major Peking Paper Declares Mao is Politically Paralyzed." Here are some eye-openers from that clipping:

> China's second most important daily newspaper has revealed that Chairman Mao Tse-tung is seriously ill and charged he is politically "paralyzed," his condition deliberately concealed by the regime.
>
> A full-page article declared that Mao had permitted a pro-capitalist group to come to power. . . .
>
> Some China specialists took the startlingly outspoken article as confirmation that the eighty-year-old chairman is suffering from the complex ailment called Parkinsonism.
>
> . . . the Communist regime could perish in the second generation after Mao. . . .

One of his closing speeches in 1974 was a thirty-seven-point "self review" in which he admitted his political judgment was not infallible.

Mao was a five-time loser. He lost his chairmanship, his presidency, his health, his hold on the people, and his face.

Solomon was right when he stated in Proverbs that the way that seems right to men is a dead end (Proverbs 16:25).

A Nation Bewildered

How has all this affected the mainland Chinese? What is the result of such bankruptcy? Well, disappointment, discouragement, and disillusionment are now filling the hearts of the Chinese people. Especially the young, which makes up half of China's 800 million. They have come to the cold realization through the bare facts that the answer to their problems does not lie in Mao Tse-tung or any Communist ideology. It lies somewhere else.

As much as they love their homeland and families, they are willing to sacrifice all that in their desperate search for answers.

During my last two visits to the Orient, I learned the British Crown Colony estimated about 10 thousand freedom swimmers arrive there each year. They are the lucky ones, for Hong Kong's official computer figures only one in four succeeds[26] while the PLA claims they capture or kill five out of every six who try to escape.

Two young Christian fishermen I spoke to, while boating to Duck Island off China's coast, told me they continually discover floating corpses on the open sea. They said sometimes the bodies would come so close to their fishing boat they could stoop down and touch them.

The younger one told me once an engaged couple decided to escape. Unfortunately, en route the boy got sick and died. The young lady, being a very determined person, pushed, dragged, and carried the body of her fiancé over the mountain and across the water until she reached the other side, the "promised land."

Why are they so dissatisfied they risk their lives to get out? Obviously Communism has failed to meet the individual's needs. Mao's way of building Utopia without God is like making egg rolls without the eggs and chicken chow mein with no chicken.

Food Stamps Chinese Style

Communism has had a quarter century to prove itself in China. Although it has become a nuclear power and taken a seat among the nations, how is mister average Chinese faring? Is there a chicken in every pot? Have they outlawed crime?

Some say the citizens in China today can leave their doors unlocked at night without fear of burglary. They claim that if your purse or wallet is lost in the streets, not a penny would be removed from it. Others brag that there is no prostitution, no problem with beggars, and no lack of food or housing.

Are these statements accurate? Have they achieved Utopia? Or has the picture been taken with a rose-colored lens? Do they really illustrate the overall situation behind the Bamboo Curtain?

A friend of mine in Fukien told me food is strictly rationed. He said the amount of rice allotted for each person per month can vary from four to thirteen kilos. This is roughly nine to twenty-eight pounds a month or .3 to .93 pounds a day. When you consider that one pound of rice can fill seven and a half bowls (smaller than the average cereal bowls) when cooked and a hard-working male adult needs at least three bowls per meal, you can see the average of 18.8 pounds a month rice supply is grossly inadequate.

This is why Mrs. Wakabayashi, who lived in China for twenty-two years under Communism, stated in her interview with *U. S. News & World Report* that they ate ground corn dumplings and salt soup (boiling water with a few vegetables) for breakfast. Dinner usually consisted of corn millet or sorghum gruel with "white tea" (which was nothing more than hot water). She told the interviewer they could only afford meat or fish three times a year.[27] No wonder peasants often have to satisfy their hunger with wild vegetation.

Food is not the only commodity to be rationed. Each person is allowed only fourteen feet of cloth per year—that's less than five yards! The purchase of socks, towels, and underwear all require coupons as well.

It is also reported that the people inside cannot buy high quality goods, medicines, or fruits. They can only select from third-class things because the best items are exported.

Those who sympathize with the Communist government argue that the rationing program is necessary because of the tremendous number of mouths to feed. But is this reasoning valid? Let's look at the other side of the coin. The huge population also offers the regime fantastic amounts of brains and brawn. Imagine what a tremendous resource this is. If properly motivated and utilized, it can be the greatest strength in the world. The Chinese people are not stupid or lazy. They have proven themselves in Hong Kong, Taiwan, Philippines, United States, and many other parts of the world. If the 15 million Chinese on the little island of Formosa and the 4 million on the tiny British colony can earn a good living, why can't the folks on the mainland do the same? Obviously the problem is the system, not the people. Communism has advanced the state— but it has been at the expense of the people. Instead of meat on the table, they have a mushroom cloud on the horizon. The price has certainly been "sky-high."

A couple years ago, while my relative was traveling by train toward Shanghai to reunite with her kinfolk, she noticed vegetables lying along the roadway. When she inquired about it to an officer on board, he replied, "We have such a surplus this year, there is no need to harvest them all."

After checking into the special hotel for overseas visitors, she invited her relatives to join her for a noon meal. Not only did they accept her invitation and eat heartily, they hung around to make sure that dinner was included.

Several days later she was getting a little tired of the same vegetable every day and requested a change. To her astonishment, the waiter told her there was a shortage and she was lucky to have any. Then she began to understand why her relatives enjoyed eating at the hotel so much. When they said it was the best food they had in a long time, they weren't just being polite. She rebuked herself for having been so easily deceived by the officer on the train.

Even after this rude awakening, she wasn't prepared for the shocking situation at the home of one of her family members she visited. There she found three generations, eight people in all, living in a single 10′ × 12′ room. She said to me, "I couldn't believe how grandmother, two couples, and three children live, sleep, and eat in such cramped quarters." When she complained to the local authorities they said, "We sympathize with you, but we can't help. There are such rooms occupied by four generations."

On another occasion, a friend of mine took his family for a visit to China. He saw beggars in several provinces, many waiting around for their leftovers by the restaurant entrances.

In the book, *Heavenly Revenge* by Ling Gunn, he reports how his fellow Red Guards visited the prostitutes in Hangchow while making their way up to Peking. It is apparent that this vice has not been eliminated.

Robbery is still a problem as well. A lady and her daughter testified upon their return from the mainland that young delinquents, mostly ex-Red Guards, make a habit of stealing whatever they can.

Testimonies like these are not unique. The same message is often heard from refugees who have risked life and limb to get out. The figures may vary, but the picture is the same.

Two months ago, I had the opportunity of interviewing a former Red Guard who had recently escaped from China. I want to share this experience with you for two reasons. First, he represents the typical Chinese because he is twenty-four years old and that is about the average age on the mainland. Second, he portrays perfectly the product of revolution. Here is a summary of his story:

> I was born in Canton in 1951 to a Christian family and was baptized as a baby. When the church came under attack, my parents quit going altogether.
>
> I was schooled in the thoughts of Mao and was quite active in the cultural revolution making "big character" posters.
>
> When the revolution ended and we were ordered back to the classrooms, my friends and I were very disillusioned. We realized that we had been used by Mao Tse-tung himself.
>
> Later we were sent to the countryside to work with the farmers and join the communal system. I had to get up at 4:30 in the morning to fix my own breakfast and get off to

work in the fields until 10:00. At 12:00 when lunch was over, I continued my work until 6:00.

The long hours and hard labor increased our hatred for Mao. We used to curse him out loud when no one was listening. I had no future and my life would be controlled by the Party.

When I finally got some free time, it was usually spent listening to the radio. I was lucky because I was the only one that had a radio in the whole commune.

Other times, we spent our leisure moments in cardplaying—a most popular pastime in China. We didn't play for money, so the loser had to clip a clothespin on his chin for each loss.

We were so discouraged with our lot in life and disappointed in the government that many of us decided to escape if possible. Some friends of mine tried four, five, or even six times to get out and failed.

The first two times I tried to leave ended in imprisonment. In spite of brainwashing, horrible food, sleeping with bedbugs, and hard labor, I tried for the third time—and made it.

Young people in my province, particularly, are very restless and superstitious. One time thousands of kids climbed up a hill and flew protest kites which had words like "get out of the mainland" and "escape to Hong Kong" written on their long tails.

Before one of us tries to escape, we usually want a good-luck charm such as a picture or small image of Buddha to insure success and good fortune. Sometimes we went to the ancestors' tombs and prayed to them for assistance. I got out because the spirit of my dead grandfather helped me.

A Case in Point

Inspired by his experience and apparent rejection of the Marxist-Leninist dogma, I asked him whether or not he would have accepted a gospel pamphlet or tract if someone had offered one to him. He replied, "I most definitely would. I needed something other than the Communist propaganda to read." I pressed one step further, "Supposing someone took the same booklet to a friend of yours and told him he could find his answers and solve his problems by reading it, do you think he would welcome it?" Again he affirmatively guaranteed a positive response.

As I looked into his eyes, trying to sense what he was feeling, I inquired again, "Suppose someone approached you in the commune and told you that Jesus Christ died for you and you could be saved by believing in Him, would you have accepted that invitation?"

A flash of the light of sincerity captivated his face as he answered: "You bet your life I would! I was so desperate that I went to my dead grandfather for help. It would have been good news indeed. I would have been thrilled to learn the God of heaven and earth cared for my plight."

You should have seen how excited I was as I soaked in every word he said. I couldn't wait to ask him to receive Jesus Christ as his personal Saviour and attend church regularly. With my heart full of thanksgiving and rejoicing, I left a gospel portion in his hand and drove home. It was one of those "cloud nine" experiences for me. I was most anxious to share the thrill with my co-workers. It blew my mind to meditate on the mercifulness of God. I praised Him all the way to the office for the way He has prepared a large percentage of people behind the Bamboo Curtain for the presentation of the gospel. I thanked Him most sincerely for allowing me a glimpse of that glorious future.

Surely God will call out a people to His name in spite of the atheistic blockage. Why don't you join me in a special prayer right now thanking Him for what He has done. Let us ask our wonderful victorious Lord to open the way for a harvest of souls in the mainland.

The Bible says in Psalms 22:24:

> For he hath not despised nor abhorred the affliction of the afflicted; neither hath he hid his face from him; but when he cried unto him, he heard.

7

The Dragon Changes Spots

*. . . there is no power but of God: the powers that be are
ordained of God.*

Romans 13:1

*The king's heart is in the hand of the Lord, as the rivers
of water: he turneth it whithersoever he will.*

Proverbs 21:1

Since the dawn of the 70s China has undergone dramatic
changes. A quick look at the following newspaper and magazine
headlines is sufficient proof:

In the *U. S. News & World Report*
"Close-up of Red China—Now a Real Leap Forward" Feb.
1971
"Breakthrough with China: The Meaning" July 1971
"New Shape of Asia" Mar. 1972

In two Hong Kong papers
"Security on Chinese Border Eases"
                            South China Morning Post Oct. 1971
"Outflow from China Greater Than Ever"
                            Sunday Post Herald Sept. 1971

In the *Los Angeles Herald-Examiner*
"Peking Diplomats To Get Red Carpet Treatment" Nov.
1971
"Nixon Meets Mao" Feb. 1972
"Secret Agreement With China" Feb. 1972

"Russia, Chinese Rivalry Widens" Jan. 1973
"A Change in China" (editorial) Feb. 1973
"New U.S.—China Tie" Feb. 1973

For more than twenty years the Middle Kingdom has kept her doors to the free world tightly closed and bolted. Why the sudden change? What caused the about-face? And how does all this fit into God's plan for the Church hidden behind the Bamboo Curtain?

The Cause

At least two major developments forced China to warm up to the free world. First of all, serious troubles developed with the USSR, who had been supplying her with technical advice and economic assistance. Here's why.

Things hadn't gone well for China ever since her "big brother" laughed at the failures of the Great Leap Forward and withdrew their support. Their alliance deteriorated quickly in the early 1960s as their ideological rift became more evident. In 1962 China openly condemned Russia for bending under U. S. pressure and withdrawing the missiles from Cuba. Peking claimed that the only way to overthrow capitalism, their basic goal, was through aggression and revolution. (They will eat these words a decade later!) Mao accused Khrushchev of modern revisionism and being a traitor to Marxist-Leninist ideals.

This Sino-Soviet feud reminds me of the story of two boys engaged in a bitter argument. The little one finally became so frustrated that he yelled, "I'll bet my dad could beat up your dad if we weren't brothers!"

Fighting erupted along the 4,000-mile border between the two Communist brothers. As the situation became more and more threatening, negotiations and defense build-up took place simultaneously.

Since they got nowhere at the peace table, they both continued sending troops to the front. By 1973 Russia had deployed one-fourth of her 164-division army and a quarter of the 45 hundred planes along the frontier. In turn, China increased its battle array by more than 30 percent to include up to forty-five divisions, thus making the China-Soviet border the most heavily guarded in the world.

Even so, the dragon was getting scared out of its skin. China knew that in case of all-out war with her nuclear-powered neighbor, she wouldn't have a prayer (pun intended).

With no hope of reconciliation and the ever-increasing fear of being attacked, Peking was desperate for new friends to use as benefactors.

The Russian threat wasn't the only motivation for China's change of attitude toward the West. There were internal reasons as well.

To begin with, Mao's failures demanded a change of leadership. As the aging dictator was being phased out, his radical "closed-door policy" toward the free world became obsolete, too.

After the disastrous Cultural Revolution the power structure began shifting to the moderates. Military men flooded into the new Central Committee. (It is interesting that the published list of Central Committee members reveals 45 percent as PLA officers, 40 percent CCP veterans, and only 5 percent radical Maoists.) This is a dramatic change when you consider the 1954 State Constitution made no mention of the PLA's primacy. But now the PLA has become the solid cornerstone of the Chinese power structure.

What is so significant about this?

These military leaders were obsessed with Russia to the point of being paranoid. Their main concern wasn't pursuing ideological goals, but rather in methods of strengthening the country. They discarded Mao's old-fashioned concept of building a strong nation by using the backs of the peasants alone.

In order to advance herself from the thirteenth economic position in the world, upgrade her educational system, gain international recognition and influence, improve her technology, and eliminate the Soviet threat, they had to rejoin the world.

The Bamboo Curtain was virtually forced to open in 1971. Was God directing all this behind the scene? You bet your life! Everything was precisely on schedule according to God's time-table.

The Effects

China made a genuine great leap forward in 1971 when her envoys arrived in New York to claim their new United Nations seat. Twenty-two years of frustrated attempts to replace the Republic of China (Taiwan) in the United Nations finally paid off as the red carpet was rolled out for them. This significant dramatic change is the beginning of many things to come.

On February 20, 1972, Henry Kissinger returned from an extensive four-day conference in Peking. He had successfully paved the way for the historical visit of Richard Nixon. For the first time since the Communist takeover, the East met the West. On February 21, Mao and Nixon shook hands as the world looked on.

The Bamboo Curtain opened wider to accommodate the increasing foreign trade. By the end of this year of Ping-Pong diplomacy, China's dealings with Japan approached $1 billion making her the first among all trading partners.

For the first time, the United States was open for business with the People's Republic. Agreements were made for China to purchase half a million tons of wheat, ten Boeing 707 jetliners, and about $30 million worth of highly specialized communications equipment. In turn, American firms contracted to buy $50 million worth of Chinese chemicals, gourmet food items, furniture, and clothing.

However, the new trade agreements were not the most fascinating events during this year. The little-noticed diplomatic changes are most interesting. During 1972 foreign ministers from all major West European lands visited Peking. Yet not a single East European statesman was received. What was going on? Why was China warming up to the non-Communist countries?

Here is her strategy. If she could influence Russia's foes to form a more united front against Russia, instead of easing off as it was intending, the USSR would be too busy to cause her trouble.

Furthermore the Chinese ambassadors who had been called back during the Cultural Revolution were sent back to their overseas posts. New liaison offices were opened in May of 1973 between Washington and Peking.

To accommodate all the new traffic across China's borders, the Travel and Tourism Administration Bureau was resurrected. Newspapermen in Hong Kong were informed that modern tourist facilities were being erected in Shunchun near Kowloon.

In anticipation of an even greater influx of businessmen and tourists, China is planning a massive expansion of civil aviation routes. She purchased fifteen British Trident jetliners to add to her fleet of thirty aircraft. These new planes, which cost more than $150 million, will fly on new international routes.

The New Trio

A surprising announcement was made by Peking in February of 1975. A civilian by the name of Teng Hsiao-ping was named as the new Army Chief of Staff, making him the head of the PLA. The seventy-year-old Teng is the same fellow who was purged during the Cultural Revolution for being a "renegade." He was stripped of his posts as Party General Secretary and Second Deputy Premier and castigated as a bourgeois because he opposed Mao's radicalism.

This man, who replaced Mao as chairman of the Party Secretariat in 1956, is now elevated to the influential Party Politburo. Even though he stands just five feet tall, he's a big man in China. Seven of the eleven army commanders are his former subordinates and there's no telling how far he can go. Keep your eyes on this chap.

Teng, the ever popular newly re-elected Premier Chou En-lai, and the Defense Minister Marshal Yeh Chien-ying (Lin Piao's successor) form the new power trio. They are charting the course for the 800 million; and you can be sure it's going to be quite different from Mao's radical moves. They'll sing a new tune.

How do we know this? Just a few months ago when China convened its National People's Congress (first one in ten years!) the regime's founding father wasn't even there. This is the first time Mao was absent—whether boycotting the session or barred from it is not certain. Moreover, his name was hardly mentioned. (Only five times, to be exact.)

This meeting, held in January of 1975, was aimed at the official approval of top-level decisions regarding the future shape of China. It was a resounding victory for the moderate pragmatists.

Revival of Religion

The new relationship between China and the rest of the world had such far-reaching ramifications that it was bound to affect the Church within her borders.

In order to accommodate visiting dignitaries and maintain the facade of religious freedom, a few "showcase" churches were renovated and reopened for business.

As far back as 1971, Ada Princigalli, the new Peking correspondent for the Italian News Agency, reported she attended a Latin mass in Peking. Accompanied by two Italian government officials, she attended the service in the Spanish-style church which was conducted by Reverend Wang Ki-ting. The thirty-year-old priest identified himself as the Roman Catholic Vicar General of Peking. Sporting the clerical collar under his tunic, he told her the church was open daily for worship.

According to the *Hong Kong Standard*, two more churches (one Protestant, one Catholic) opened in October under the directorship of the Chinese Association of Religious Bureaus.

Another Hong Kong paper, the *Gong Shung Daily*, reported that Christmas carols were heard in Peking for the first time since the Cultural Revolution. A forty-five member international choir, representing eleven countries, performed the hymn, "Silent Night."

The Protestant church on Rice Market Street, which was used as a meeting hall for twelve years, was reopened under the direction of the Peking Union Theological Seminary. Joint Anglican-Protestant services were held each Sunday. It is also said that a few churches in Chekiang were reopened in this same year.

Donald Mackay reported in the *Hong Kong Standard* that a small Catholic Church of the Virgin Mary and an even smaller Protestant church reopened in Peking, basically to serve the growing diplomatic corps. (He is obviously referring to the ones we have already mentioned.) In his report he said the services were conducted in Latin with a choir and a Chinese priest; only a handful of elderly Chinese had attended the meetings.

Mackay went on to say that only about a half dozen of the local people attended the services at the Protestant church where a white-haired Chinese woman played Western hymns on a piano.

These two churches were intended to serve the fifty diplomatic missions involving seven hundred foreigners living in a city of seven million people. The *New York Times* reported the two churches were crowded on July 9 for the first time since the start of the Cultural Revolution. The article further stated: About forty students attended a Protestant service in an old style Chinese hall.[28] Apparently, the paper was referring to the hall located just north of Peking's main street, the Avenue of Eternal Tranquility.

Another visitor, Rene Q. Bas, related her experience after attending a mass in Peking. She said it was in Latin and followed the old liturgy. The church was laid out in the same form as any Roman Catholic Church with the altar being dominated by a magnificent painting of Mary. From her conversation with the Bishop, she learned that the church had no tie with the Vatican because of its imperialistic connections. Interestingly, he added that he and the ten other priests of the church worked in the toy and handicraft industry during the week.

There is obviously a sort of religious detente situation on the mainland. The new moderate regime has had to take a more compromising stance in order to maintain the facade of religious freedom. In keeping with that, some Buddhist temples have reopened, such as Lam Chuan Temple in Changchow and Lam Po Tot in Amoy.

The Underground Church

While the policy changes brought about the opening of the registered churches, it lessened the pressure on the clandestine cell groups. Before this era of change enveloped China, particularly during the Cultural Revolution, Christians who dared to meet secretly for worship took great risks. Today, however, they can meet in a more open fashion. Reports have claimed that even Communist officers, the ones they tried to hide from, have shown up in such meetings occasionally.

Several months ago a personal friend of mine returned from a visit to Foochow on the mainland. He told me about the conversion of a Communist officer. Let me share this remarkable true story with you.

It all began when the officer's daughter became very seriously ill (they believed she was possessed by an evil spirit). In his desperation for his child's cure, he secretly begged an idol to heal her. Later he was told the only way to rid the girl of the demon was to put her on his back and crawl down the street on his knees until they bled. After this public display of humility and penance, the child got worse instead of better.

When the incident reached the ears of some Christians, they invited the official to their secret service where they told him the Good News of the gospel. The man believed in Jesus Christ and accepted Him as his personal Saviour. He knelt and begged for forgiveness of sins and the healing of his daughter.

Upon returning home that day, he discovered that his child was healed. Since then he went around rejoicing and telling his co-workers about the Lord. He said, "Even if the authorities threaten to behead me, I will never deny God."

Many new souls were added to the kingdom because of his powerful testimony.

Another example of the more relaxed atmosphere among believers is illustrated by this account. A couple who are members of the church I pastored in Los Angeles took a trip to Canton last year. During their stay there, they invited all the relatives and friends for a reunion dinner. Since they were forewarned by many not to speak about religious things, they decided to dispense with the open prayer of thanks for the food. However, before they could poise their chopsticks, an elderly lady blurted out, "Wait a minute. We don't want to start eating just like this. We must thank God for this abundance of wonderful food."

Although they all paused for the moment of prayer offered by the brave old lady, many of the unsaved guests made it known that it was unnecessary and a little bit crazy.

The public witness of the officer and the prayer of the elderly lady clearly demonstrate the new mood within the semi-clandestine body of believers in the Middle Kingdom today.

Border Restrictions Eased

It's no secret that security along the border between China and Hong Kong has eased up quite a bit since the beginning of the 70s. According to an article in the *Los Angeles Times* on November 11, 1973, about 7,000 Chinese with legal exit visas crossed the border into Hong Kong in October, and 2,191 crossed in the first five days of November. The *South China Morning Post* carried an article in October of 1971 on this very subject. Here are a couple excerpts from it:

> News of lax security by frontier guards of the People's Liberation Army has spread to many parts of China, prompting a large number of youths to plan escapes to Hong Kong.
>
> The guards have recently ceased to shoot at escapees sighted along the waterways bordering Hong Kong, according to an arrival from China.[29]

One escapee claimed he came face to face with a patrol officer just when he was about to jump into the water to make his bid for freedom. To his joyful astonishment, the guard pretended he didn't see him and turned away.

Security has eased up for those entering China also. A few years ago it was impossible to openly carry a Bible or any Christian literature across the border. When immigration officers discovered such items, they would ask you to leave it with them and pick it up on your way out.

But lately things have changed. Many tourists have been allowed to take a Bible or two and some Christian literature without any problems. Millions of overseas Chinese have visited China.

A friend of mine, who made two trips to China within the last year, was permitted to take two Christian booklets out of the six he carried on the first trip, and ten out of twelve on the second one.

Reappearance of the Word

Obviously those who are taking advantage of the government's more relaxed policy are able to leave Christian literature, gospel booklets, and Bibles in the waiting hands of mainlanders. I personally have talked to overseas Chinese who have done this. It is thrilling to see how God is answering the prayers of His saints on both sides of the Bamboo Curtain. Those who take the Bibles in and those who receive them express a divine joy that is indescribable.

A young mother recently visited her relatives on the mainland and left her personal gold-edged Bible with one couple. She told me how tears filled their eyes as they thanked the Lord for answered prayer. They had prayed for many years for such a treasure.

I don't know about you, but I feel shame that I have not taken full advantage of the freedom to own and read the Word of God. It's too bad that we don't fully appreciate a privilege until we lose it. May God help us to treasure His Word more.

What you have witnessed so far is a direct result of the change in policy. There was a time when the Word of God was a most dangerous Book to own. A while ago I spoke to an elderly couple in New York who had just come out from Shanghai. They recalled how they tried to hide their own Bible during the Cultural Revolution for fear of persecution.

By contrast, in the article "The Bible in Modern Chinese," David Watson pointed out that a small number of Bibles are now circulating openly in Canton. Some are seen in private homes and in the marketplaces. According to him, Christian groups are now being allowed to worship in private homes in a few large cities.

In a meeting of the "China Group" mission leaders within the evangelical and interdenominational Foreign Missions Associations, Gorden Bell (FEBC Representative), Don MacInnis (experienced China-watcher), and Ed Torjensen (Radio Taiwan representative) gave encouraging reports of open worship assemblies in remote areas. However, Torjensen pointed out that the incidents were far removed from Peking, taking place mostly in the southwest and Canton.

On the Mark . . . Get Set. . . .

It is not my intention to give you the impression that China has genuinely changed toward Christians or our God. The turnabout has been forced upon them due to circumstances beyond their control. We know who is causing this to happen, don't we!

Isaiah 52:10 has this to say:

> The Lord hath made bare his holy arm in the eyes of all the nations; and all the ends of the earth shall see the salvation of our God.

The Bible is saying here that the Lord has "rolled up His sleeves" in the eyes of all the nations—which includes the Communist powers—to get the job done. When it says all the ends of the earth shall see His salvation, it naturally includes China.

God has shaken up the government to such an extent they've had to ease off on the Church. However, let's not be misled by this dramatic change into thinking there's any red-carpet treatment in store for missionaries in the near future. There isn't.

But don't despair. Evangelism is not at a standstill. Our brothers and sisters who have endured the fiery trials and graduated from God's school of purification are more than ready to carry on the work of evangelism. Under the guidance and power of the Holy Spirit, the sky's the limit!

A Chinese merchant of Indonesia who visited Fukien province twice in 1973 gives this personal account:

> Hundreds of pagans and entire villages have been won or won back to the Christian faith.

(This again substantiates the dramatic conversion story mentioned in the beginning of this book, doesn't it?)

Praise the Lord! He has prepared China religiously, spiritually, linguistically, psychologically, and governmentally for a massive evangelism program to take place speedily.

Remember what Jesus said as recorded in John 4:35?

> Say not ye, There are yet four months, and then cometh harvest? behold, I say unto you, Lift up your eyes, and look on the fields; for they are white already to harvest.

8

Pressing Toward the Mark

. . . pray ye therefore the Lord of the harvest, that he would send forth labourers into his harvest.

Luke 10:2

Sometime in the near future, both before and after the rapture of the Church, hundreds of thousands will come to know the Lord in China.

This future revival will be unparalleled. It's going to be something that the Middle Kingdom has never seen before.

How could this help but happen. It's inevitable!

Why?

To begin with, the nature of God demands it. His attribute of love guarantees that He will not ignore a quarter of mankind. Definitely a percentage exceeding by far the fractional figure in 1949 will be counted for the kingdom.

Next, the nature of Communism necessitates it. Nothing proves the personal need for God more quickly and effectively than trying to live without Him. For the past two and a half decades, God has allowed Peking to deny the people any normal spiritual outlet. He has permitted the Reds to replace religion with Maoism. Furthermore, He tolerated the regime's assault on the masses. What for? Only to point out the bankruptcy of atheism and the undeniable spiritual vacuum within man.

Finally, the nature of divine preparation compels it. God has given Christianity an even footing, made it indigenous, and erased denominational lines. His children have been purified and taught the lessons of complete trust and dependance upon Him. He has sharpened the evangelistic tools by simplifying and unifying the written and spoken language. And the people have experienced for themselves that to deny God's existence is to rob their own lives of value and hope.

Can you see the wisdom of our God in allowing China to be captured by Communism?

The stage has been set for the drama. The Bamboo Curtain is lifting. The Lamb has victoriously forced open the dragon's den.

The Prophetic Picture

In spite of the official compromises being made, Communism will never honestly change its position toward God. The official Party magazine, *Red Flag*, makes it clear:

> We must combat religion—this goal is the ABCs of materialism and therefore of Marxism.

Notwithstanding, God is governing its purpose. They may make ripples and even waves on the sea of humanity, but God is the One controlling the current and the flow. Proverbs 16:9 makes it clear.

Look at the course already charted for mankind as found in God's prophetic Word. We know that out of the 800 million on the mainland, some will be caught up to be with the Lord when He comes for His Church in the rapture. However, the large majority will be left behind for the darkest age the world has ever seen—the Great Tribulation.

Revelation 16 says that during this seven-year period, China will send 200 million soldiers to the Middle East for battle. Before they are destroyed along with the forces of the Antichrist, they will destroy one-third of mankind. Most likely, this will be accomplished with ICBMs. For as early as 1969, the Bulletin of Atomic Scientists reported that China was striving for an ICBM capability.[30]

The war will escalate until the very existence of man is threatened. Revelation 16:19 says that the cities of the nations will be destroyed.

Here is an interesting footnote. Among the three biggest powers in the world, China would be the least hurt in a nuclear confrontation. Why? Because her population distribution makes her the least vulnerable in such a war. You see, only 15 percent of China's masses live in cities big enough to qualify as potentially worthwhile nuclear warhead targets. Yet 73 percent of the Americans and 56 percent of the Russians live in such areas.

Can you see what I'm driving at? This means the most populous nation on earth will suffer the least casualties. And the survivors of this devastating holocaust who will be ushered into God's Kingdom Age (when Christ reigns for a thousand years) will include a good healthy percentage of Chinese. Isn't it exciting to realize that many of the same people who are denied God under Chinese Communism will be living under Christ's personal rule? Oh, the matchless justice and mercy of the Almighty God!

Work for the Night Is Coming

The world is rushing headlong into the darkest of the dark ages. As the hands on the clock move toward midnight, the Spirit of God is moving mightily among His own, drawing the last ones into His fold.

During the past two years of traveling to many parts of the globe, I have seen a significant and timely development among the Chinese outside the mainland. As the sense of urgency and winds of revival gain magnitude, they are increasingly burdened to pray for their brethren in China.

From March 10 through 16 of 1975, Chinese Christians in the Philippines sponsored a special "Pray for China Week." It was my privilege to witness their genuine concern and love for souls in the Middle Kingdom.

The impact of this international first-time demonstration of love and concern was felt keenly in Hong Kong and Formosa especially.

It is heartwarming that Chinese Christians in the free world are becoming more and more concerned for their mainland counterparts. I believe this is also in God's plan because they are the best equipped and most qualified candidates to assist the Church behind the Bamboo Curtain. They can play a vital supporting role by praying and taking in Bibles. The tools they supply will arm the God-trained mainland soldiers of the Cross to carry on an unprecedented evangelistic effort to hasten the hundred-fold harvest.

Small wonder Oscar Buck feels the future of Christianity will not be determined in Africa, Europe, or America—it will be determined in the Orient.

Dr. Abraham Kuyper, former Prime Minister of Holland and noted theologian predicts:

> The Asiatic question is in fact of most serious import. The problem of the world took its rise in Asia, and in Asia will find its final solution.

Arnold Toynbee says the twenty-first century will belong to China.

The Chinese will definitely play a major role in God's plans. They will carry the torch and finish the last evangelistic lap around the world.

The seeds sown a long time ago in China have been multiplying these past twenty-five years in the soil fertilized by the martyred saints. Nourished by the water of purification, pruned by the ax of atheism, and strengthened by the life-giving Son-Light, the Church has grown to maturity. It is invincible. Fear can't finish it; regimentation can't reverse it; intimidation can't invert or inter it; denunciation can't demolish it; imprisonment can't inhibit it; isolation can't impede it; persecution can't prevail against it; brainwashing can't budge it; reeducation can't ruin it; enslavement can't exterminate or extirpate it; massacre can't mar it and darkness cannot damage it.

For the past quarter of a century, the Lord has been preparing the Middle Kingdom religiously, spiritually, linguistically, psychologically, and governmentally for a massive evangelism program yet to be seen by the world. The Holy Spirit Himself has wrought a wonderful work upon the Chinese Christians and shaped them into soldiers of the Cross.

This army of God marches on victoriously toward the fifth and no doubt final major evangelistic movement in China to reap a hundred-fold harvest.

Onward, Christian soldiers!

Notes

1. *Peking Review,* October 4, 1974 (Peking).
2. Hudson Taylor, *To China . . . With Love* (Denville, N. J.: Dimension Books, Inc.).
3. Francis Price Jones, ed., *Documents of the Three-Self Movement* (National Council of Churches, East Asia Dept. 1963).
4. George N. Patterson, *Christianity in Communist China* (Waco, Texas: Word, Inc., 1969).
5. Francis Price Jones, *The Church in Communist China* (New York: Friendship Press, 1962), pp. 53–55.
6. Hsing-yao Hsieh, "Historical Survey of Mission Work in China," *Current Background* #68 (Hong Kong: U. S. Consulate General).
7. *China News Service,* August 13, 1954 (Peking).
8. Jones, *The Church in Communist China,* pp. 82–85.
9. Ibid., pp. 156, 157.
10. *Hong Kong Tiger Standard,* December 3, 1962 (Hong Kong).
11. Richard L. Walker, *The Human Cost of Communism in China* (Washington: U. S. Government Printing Office, 1971).
12. Harold H. Martinson, *Red Dragon Over China* (Minneapolis: Augsburg Publishing House, 1956).
13. Jones, *The Church in Communist China,* p. 67.
14. *The New Republic,* May 13, 1957 (Washington).
15. Patterson, *Christianity in Communist China.*
16. Leslie T. Lyall, *Come Wind, Come Weather* (Chicago: Moody Press, 1960), pp. 45, 46, 48.

17. Jones, *The Church in Communist China*, p. 105.
18. *Life*, October 7, 1966 (New York).
19. *China Notes*, July 1967.
20. *Human Events*, June 7, 1975 (Washington).
21. *Collected Documents of the First National Conference on the Reform of the Chinese Script* (Peking: 1957).
22. Chou En-lai, *The Task Confronting Us in Language and Script Reform* (Peking: 1958).
23. Mary Wang, *The Chinese Church That Will Not Die* (Wheaton: Tyndale House Publishers, 1972).
24. Ling Gunn, *The Heavenly Revenge* (Hong Kong: Sun Ging Company, 1972).
25. Ibid.
26. *South China Morning Post*, December 1973.
27. *U. S. News & World Report*, February 15, 1971 (Washington).
28. *The New York Times*, July 10, 1972 (New York).
29. *South China Morning Post*, October 1971.
30. Michael Yahuda, "China's Nuclear Options," *Bulletin of the Atomic Scientists* (Chicago: February 1969).